Y0-AGJ-061

BOLLINGEN SERIES IX

On the

ILIAD

by

RACHEL BESPALOFF

TRANSLATED FROM THE FRENCH BY
MARY McCARTHY

INTRODUCTION BY
HERMANN BROCH

BOLLINGEN SERIES IX

PRINCETON UNIVERSITY PRESS

Copyright 1947 by Bollingen Foundation, Washington, D.C.
Published by Princeton University Press, Princeton, N.J.

THIS VOLUME IS THE NINTH IN A
SERIES OF BOOKS SPONSORED BY
BOLLINGEN FOUNDATION

First Princeton/Bollingen Paperback printing, 1970
Second hardcover printing, 1970

ISBN 0-691-01769-7 (paperback edn.)
ISBN 0-691-09806-9 (hardcover edn.)

LCC 70-126833

Manufactured in the United States of America

CONTENTS

THE STYLE OF THE
MYTHICAL AGE

AN INTRODUCTION BY
HERMANN BROCH

OMEWHERE in this book Rachel Bespaloff says: "It is impossible to speak of an Homeric world or a Tolstoyan world in the sense one can speak of a Dantesque world, a Balzacian or a Dostoievskian world. Tolstoy's universe, like Homer's, is what our own is from moment to moment. We do not step into it; we are there."—This is a somewhat startling statement; and when we ask why it should be valid, one reason seems to us especially relevant: Homer is on the threshold where myth steps over into poetry, Tolstoy on that where poetry steps back into myth.

Coming from myth, returning to myth: the whole, or nearly the whole, history of European literature is strung between Homer and Tolstoy. But what a strange development of the human expression, since, apparently, it returns to its mythical source. Is this not like a late homecoming? And if it be such—does it not portend the dusk before the night? Is it not the curve that drops back into childhood?

Undoubtedly myth embraces qualities of both periods, that of childhood (so nearly identical with that of primitive man) and that of old age, the styles of both expressing the essential and nothing but the essential, the one before it has entered the realm of subjective problems, the other when it has left this realm behind.

The "style of old age" is not always a product of the years; it is a gift implanted along with his other gifts in the artist, ripening, it may be, with time, often blossoming before its season under the foreshadow of death, or unfolding of itself even before the approach of age or death: it is the reaching of a new level of expression, such as the old Titian's discovery of the all-penetrating light which dissolves the human flesh and the human soul to a higher unity; or such as the finding by Rembrandt and Goya, both at the height of their manhood, of the metaphysical surface which underlies the visible in man and thing, and which nevertheless can be painted; or such as the *Art of the Fugue* which Bach in his old age dictated without having a concrete instrument in mind, because what he had to express was either beneath or beyond the audible surface of music; or such as the last quartets of Beethoven, in which he—only then in his fifties but already near to death—found the way from earthly music to the music of the infinite; or such as Goethe's last writings, the final scenes of *Faust* for instance, where the language discloses its own mysteries and, therefore, those of all existence.

What is common to these various examples? All of them reveal a radical change in style, not merely a development in the original direction; and this sharp stylistic break can be described as a kind of *abstractism* in which the expression relies less and less on the vocabulary, which finally becomes reduced to a few prime symbols, and instead relies more and more on the syntax: for in essence this is what abstractism is—the impoverishment of vocabulary and the enrichment of the syntactical relations of expression; in mathematics the vocabulary is reduced to nothing, and the system of expression relies exclusively on the syntax.

In the complicated interplay between vocabulary and syntax, as it appears in the arts, most of the vocables are the result of syntactical combinations which become universally accepted conventions, i.e., as symbols, and as such are regarded as naturalistic representations. We have only to note the stylizations of medieval art which, as the writings of the period advise us, were then considered realistically convincing. That forming of conventional vocables, by which the "content" of the piece of art is transmitted to the spectator, the reader, the listener (procuring for him at the same time the naïve pleasure of recognizing such contents) is the basic characterization of all period styles, style being the fixing of a set of conventions for a certain epoch. Even music, the most "syntactical" of all arts and, therefore, as one would suppose, the most independent of vocable formation, shows in its styles that here, too, the same process of converting syntactical relations into a conventional vocabulary occurs of necessity again and again.

The artist thus graced and cursed with the "style of old age" is not content with the conventional vocabulary provided him by his epoch. For to render the epoch, the whole epoch, he cannot remain within it; he must find a point beyond it. This often appears to him a technical problem, the problem of dissolving the existing vocabulary and, from its syntactical roots, forming his own. His main, sometimes his sole concern is one of craftsmanship: Bach's *Art of the Fugue* was intended as a purely technical work; and the Japanese painter, Hokusai, reaching the peak of his mastery at about ninety, had only this to say: "Now at last I begin to learn how one draws a line."

But although the artist's problem seems to be mainly technical, his real impulse goes beyond this— it goes to the universe; and the true piece of art, even though it be the shortest lyric, must always embrace the totality of the world, must be the mirror of that universe, but one of full counterweight. This is felt by every true artist, but is creatively realized only by the artist of old age. The other, who remains bound to his conventional vocabulary, seduced by the known richness of its content—a Frans Hals or a Thomas Wolfe —though he may enlarge his art more and more, reaching a boundless abundance, is never able to achieve his real goal: one cannot capture the universe by snaring its atoms one by one; one can only capture it by showing its basic and essential principles, its basic, and one might even say, its mathematical structure. And here the abstractism of such ultimate principles joins hands with the abstractism of the technical problem: this union constitutes the "style of old age."

The artist who has reached such a point is beyond art. He still produces art, but all the minor and specific problems, with which art in its worldly phase usually deals, have lost interest for him; he is interested neither in the "beauty" of art, nor in the effect which it produces on the public: although more the artist than any other, his attitude approximates that of the scientist, with whom he shares the concern for expressing the universe; however, since he remains an artist, his abstractism is not that of science but—surprisingly enough—very near to that of myth. And there is deep significance in the fact that the creations of the "style of old age" acquire, for the most part, mythical character and even, as in the case of Goethe's *Faust*, have become, being so full of essential symbols, new members of mankind's mythical Pantheon.

Both myth and the "style of old age" become abbreviations of the world-content by presenting its structure, and this in its very essence.

"As for myself, I find it difficult to tell all; I am not a God," says Homer. And Rachel Bespaloff adds: These modest words of Homer could have been adopted by Tolstoy for himself. To both of them it was not necessary to express everything in order to express the Whole. They alone (and, at times, Shakespeare as well) were in possession of those planetarian pauses above the earthly happening, pauses in which history in its continuous flight beyond every human goal reveals its creative un-accomplishment." And in this never-accomplished and always self-creating reality—the building of a new vocabulary out of syntax —lies the essential.

And this explains the connection—at first surprising to us—between myth and mathematics. For every real approach of man to the universe can be called a presentiment of the infinite. Without this, not mathematics, nor myth, nor art, nor any other form of cognition would exist. "The sense of the true is always a kind of conquest, but first it is a gift," says Rachel Bespaloff.

It is this sense of truth, innate in the infinite, which compels man to build perceptive models of the world. For instance, the model of history by Marx employs such economic vocables as exploitation, concentration of capital, etc.; the vocabulary of classical physics consists of certain connotations, such as matter, force, energy, etc.; the psychological model of Freud works with the vocables of drive, suppressed desire, compulsion and the like. In all these models a picture of reality is developed by the composition of the vocables in a syntactical relationship directed by some basic logical rules. In the mythical model these "vocables" consist of the various and imperceptible forces by which primitive man feels himself threatened and moved, within and without; and they are represented by the gods and heroes, their acts and motivations, which then come to form the syntactical texture of the whole model, keeping it in motion. The mythical model is a cosmogony and a theogony ruled by a supreme authority of so remote and abstract a character that even the gods must yield to its commands, becoming merely its actors: this power is Fate. The position of Fate in respect to the mythical model is exactly the same as that of the basic logical rules in respect to the scientific model of the world. No wonder that in the later Greek philosophy Fate and Logos come to have an increasingly identical connotation.

So one returns to Aristotle's remarks on Hesiod, recognizing myth as a kind of pre-science of primitive man, his so-to-speak mathematics. For myth is the first emanation of the Logos in the human mind, in the human language; and never could the human mind or its language have conceived the Logos had not the conception been already formed in the myth. Myth is the archetype of every phenomenal cognition of which the human mind is capable.

Archetype of all human cognition, archetype of science, archetype of art—myth is consequently the archetype of philosophy too. There exists no philosophy which, in its structure and modes of thought, could not be traced back into the parent province of myth. Rachel Bespaloff shows in passing the connection between Platonism and myth; but when in her main argument she interprets Homer's metaphysical standpoint as an identification of Fate and Force— "In the *Iliad* force appears as both the supreme reality and the supreme illusion of life"—she shows implicitly that this blind force, as the nature of nature, as its inescapable law, represents a connection with the metaphysics of existentialism. Philosophy is a constant fight against the remnants of mythical thinking and a constant struggle to achieve mythical structure in a new form, a fight against the metaphysical convention and a struggle to build a new metaphysics; for metaphysics, itself bounded by myth, bounds philosophy, which without these boundaries would have no existence at all. The myth of Jacob who fought against the angel in order to be blessed by him is the myth of philosophy itself.

Myth becomes religion when the mythical model of the universe, hitherto merely cognated or expressed in certain visible forms (of art, etc.) passes into the act of man, coloring his entire behavior, influencing his daily life. In being a member of the *polis* participating in its civic duties, its religious celebrations, its mystery rites, the Greek citizen became a unit in the all-embracing cosmogony (and theogony) which was tentatively limned in his myths. And the medieval peasant, with no knowledge of reading and writing, with no knowledge of the Latin he heard in his church, nevertheless felt himself a part of the Catholic Universe by virtue of the whole hierarchy of values which mirrored the universe, and in which he belonged by living it. The civilization of an epoch is its myth in action.

In other words: civilization, in spite of its practical issues, reveals itself as an all-coordinating myth expressed in a certain vocabulary of human attitudes and actions, which have become conventional and—just for this reason—form a general (and religious) system of values structurally symbolic of the universe. The great periods of culture and their styles, of which the artistic styles are only facets, are marked by the validity of their religious systems of values; they are "closed systems," i.e., systems which cannot be enlarged, but only destroyed and revolutionarily replaced by some other.

When myth through enactment has come to be religion, then art (along with other aspects of existence) becomes of necessity the handmaid of the central religious values, its function being to resymbolize these values which symbolize the world. In this way art is relieved of the labor which otherwise would be required to build its universal structure. It is left free for other tasks, and the human individuality, at first immersed in myth, is now progressively liberated to become the preoccupation of art. The myth of Christ in the art of the Middle Ages is set amidst a landscape of intimate sweetness, of maternal love, of masculine dignity, which embraces the whole scale of human feeling. Thus, after the Dark Ages the rigid grandeur of the myth became increasingly domestic and human, as it was swathed in the charms of legend; for this is the principal means by which it is brought closer to the daily lives of the people. Art, by this means, fulfills its serving task of being educative and social. So in legend the closed system representing the myth reaches a climax of humanization; but it is still a closed system, and for precisely this reason the art of such a period (the fifteenth-century Gothic, for example) renders in full the style of the epoch and in that style, though only in the style, the epoch in its entirety.

The legend makes myth not only human but humane. Homer, however, although merging the myth with art, does not approach legend but remains austere. Nevertheless his creation is humanization and it begins at the center of the myth with Fate which, according to Rachel Bespaloff (and also to Simone Weil's coincidentally parallel essay), he identifies with Force. Yet this Force, though an anthropomorphic projection of human nature, is far from being humane; nor is Homeric Fate humane. The gods under the spell of such fate are vested with human but not humane qualities.

Indeed, Homer's humanization of the gods goes a step farther. It is true that they are not stripped of their abstract, mythical character; what they were they remain—mere names of the gigantic forces they represent, forces which keep in motion the model of the world and the struggle of man. But by transforming these impersonal qualities, which he leaves to the gods, into an element of poetic irony, Homer achieves their humanization, in a manner specifically his own.

Rachel Bespaloff is probably the first to discover the ironic light which flares up at the collision of the impersonal and the personal (that is, of myth and poetry), a light in which the gods become, as Jean Wahl expresses it, "sometimes slightly less, sometimes slightly more than the human being," so that, on the one side, they are passionately involved in the human struggle, while on the other—and that is especially true of Zeus—they are simply spectators, continuously and almost scientifically detached spectators of the whole human comedy, including even that part they themselves play in it. Against this background of cruel abstractness stands the human being: "The heroes of the *Iliad* attain their highest lucidity at a point when justice has been utterly crushed and obliterated."

The constant presence of the divine participants in the *Iliad*, this constant presence of their mythical activity, this constant sense of their remoteness and irony reduces the personal human problem, although potential in the myth, to an ephemeral and—again—nearly abstract role, so that, while it is never lost, it becomes situated at the *soi-distant* periphery of the poem, overshadowed by the terrible Fate of man, by his ultimate realities which are nothing but his longing for life and his certitude of death, both sustained in sorrow. Even the erotic element is removed to this periphery. "Helen," says Rachel Bespaloff, "walks across the *Iliad* as a penitent; misfortune and beauty are consummate in her and lend majesty to her step."

Herein lies the "great style" of the classics, which, while always being tied to the myth of the central value, never loses the flash of irony. As Rachel Bespaloff quotes Nietzsche: "To be a classic, one must have *all* the gifts and *all* the needs, but one must force them all under the same yoke."

The "great style" of Christian culture was reached in the pre-Renaissance; the time when the mystics opened the path for the Protestant revolution.

The Protestant revolution was one against the hierarchial concept of myth. As a Christian, man was still enacting this myth. But he had also discovered that this myth he must enact was none other than the creation of his own mind, a creation that God, by a direct act of grace, had imbedded in his soul. With this discovery man could renounce the outside hierarchy, for he was building up the universe within.

On this basic change of view the human personality as such attained new status. Heretofore it could be used only as an illustration of the myth itself—as legend. Now it was drawn from the periphery and, residing in the center, shaped about itself a humanistic world.

And this casts a new light on the phenomenon of the "great style" in the arts. The great style comes into being when the crust of the closed system cracks open to give birth to a new system. At this moment, when there is still vitality and security in the old system and its forms, still certitude in the myth, the new system, vitalized by hope and striving toward openness, creates its own new form—the great style. This is to be seen in Michelangelo, in the Greek cycle of Aeschylus, or in the sculptures of Olympia, works which, as Rachel Bespaloff points out, share the gravity of Homer.

The "great style" is security and revolution in one, and it lasts only as long as the revolutionary tendency is aflame, but is doomed to harden once more into a system, closed as was its predecessor.

The Protestant epoch—the Protestant universe—had its "great style" as well, actually one of the greatest in all history, that of the Dutch school in painting, of Bach and his predecessors in music, of Milton in poetry, and finally of Kant in philosophy, where we find less a style than the building of a Protestant scholasticism. And here, as before, the "great style" signalized the end of its epoch, when the now closed system of Protestantism had to be reopened by a new revolutionary act.

This verified the prophecy of Catholicism: in the eyes of the Church the Protestant revolt had been the first step in the destruction of the Western Christian unity, the first step in the heretical secularization of the human mind; and so it proved. In an irrevocable process, lasting from the eighteenth to the twentieth century, the Western structure of values lost its Christian center.

These one hundred and fifty years of disintegration have produced a certain attitude in man which is called romanticism. As long as the system of values is fully alive and its universe intact, man is able to solve his private and personal problems within the existing framework, while in times of disintegration such solution is achieved only when the universe is shaped anew for (and from) every particular case. It is precisely this necessity of building the universe up from every single case, and of course from each human soul, that is the basic characteristic of romanticism. Obviously this romantic procedure could never have come to pass without the preparation of Protestantism, by the tenets of which man's soul is linked directly with the universe and with God.

The Protestant dogma gives the human soul a far greater autonomy than does Catholicism, and in romanticism this autonomy becomes absolute. It is for this reason that romantic art, even when produced by a great artist, can no longer achieve the "great style," which always requires the validity of a universally accepted myth. For whatever universe may be built from the single instance, its validity is limited by the boundaries of the autonomous human soul; though it may be approved by a certain number of people, its general, not to speak of its eternal, validity remains insecure. Infected by this ultimate insecurity, the romantic artist acquires the characteristic attitude of longing, longing in particular for the religious unity of the past. Thus wishing to solve his problems in an absolute way, and feeling that Protestantism is largely responsible for the dangers of his situation, the romantic in his homesickness is led back to Catholicism, to find shelter in the Church.

Every true artist, aware that he must form his own universe, is in some ways a rebel, willing to shatter the closed system into which he is born. But he should realize that revolution is not enough, that he must also build anew the essential framework of the world. And just that is achieved by the style of old age; for this style, revolutionary by means of its abstractness, gains a level one can only call the super-religious. On this level stands Bach in his last works, Goethe and Beethoven as well, though they, born in a period when the religious system of values was already dissolved, had to reach the abstract by the detour of romanticism.

In moving from romanticism to the abstract they were precursors; Tolstoy was no less a precursor, even a more radical one. *War and Peace*, though it cannot be called a work of old age, clearly has left romanticism behind, anticipating the style of old age in a new and abstract model of the universe—an Homeric universe as Rachel Bespaloff has rightly discovered. But Tolstoy's radicalism did not content itself with this artistic approach to myth; in contrast to Goethe and Beethoven, who were, in spite of their human greatness, preponderantly artists, Tolstoy was striving for more: he was striving for the complete abstractism of a new theogony. For the style of old age, which in time he achieved, had another goal than the Homeric one, a goal nearer to Hesiod and Solon than to Homer, and the merging of myth and art; with a zeal akin to that of Savonarola, he aspired to radical finalities, and so withdrew from art altogether to construct his own ethical universe.

In the case of Beethoven and Goethe it was not only their personal genius (as in Bach's case) which compelled them toward a new style, they were enjoined to it by their epoch, in which the closed values were already being shattered. There is a fair possibility that Homer, too, felt some such command from his epoch. Cretan civilization, we know, was a late and mature one. The Geometric vases of its early period hint at a closed system, religious in nature—a medieval hierarchy of values. But the "Saffron Gatherer" of the eighteenth century B.C. already indicates the free naturalistic culture of a ripening age, characterized by the liberation of human personality, and the following period is that of the luxurious palace of Knossos, contemporaneous with the romantic mysticism of Ikhnaton's Egypt. The Eastern Mediterranean was bound in a network of commerce and trade: it was as much an age of aesthetic sophistication and of the personal problem as the later Roman period. Late Minoan art shows refined types of a highly developed court civilization—was not Trojan Paris one of them? —and bears indubitable marks of a romantic period in which the beginning of the end shows its first symptoms.

The realization of this tragic situation came with the onslaught of the Achaians. If the *Iliad* be basically Cretan in origin, it is from this dread encounter that it received its mythical shape. It is specifically mythical that the two types of the old and the new, Paris and Hector, the one a playboy and the other a patriot, should be presented as coeval and brothers. Hector, "man and among men a prince," is subject to the apocalyptic mood of his time and, therefore, affectionately recognizes the peaceful achievements of the civilization for which he is ready to fight and to die. As later in Tolstoy, the personal problems fade away, and in the rising contours of the new myth the human element is reduced to sorrow and mourning, both sober and unromantic, but great as Fate itself.

It is unlikely that Homer was Cretan; the surge of the poem is Achaian: its impact is the same as that of the first Greek carvings, not at all like those of the late Cretan period. However, it is unimaginable without the Cretan influence: were the sources of the poem purely Greek, it would exult far more than it does in the Grecian victory; only Cretan influence makes Homer's impartiality credible, an impartiality which diminishes his joy for the Greeks and balances it by his lament for the Trojans. "Call him Achilles or Hector, the conqueror is like all conquerors, and the conquered like all the conquered." Moreover, this impartiality is an aesthetic one not only on the part of the gods (whose impartiality is not justice), or on the part of the poet, but on that of his characters as well. Rachel Bespaloff, in one of her most impressive passages, interprets the meeting of Priam and Achilles who achieve a moment of kinship through their mutual recognition of each other's beauty. And let us not forget that it was beauty, Helen's beauty, which gave life to the whole conflict.

This exaltation of the aesthetic, doubtless of Cretan origin, and originally strange to the barbarian Greeks, took a marvelous hold on them. In an astonishingly short time, they wrought from it a new and Hellenic form. Out of the broken fragments of the Cretan world was developed the poetic myth which became the religion and life of the Greek world.

Whether Homer existed or not, he is described as a very old man, blind as Milton, blind as Bach, blind as Fate; the style of old age in all its greatness, coolness, and abstract transparency is so obvious in his work that people had necessarily to conceive him in this form. He himself became myth, and since behind almost every myth stands some historical reality, we ought not to ask whether he existed or not, but should simply accept him as the mythical old man, the eternal paradigm of an epoch which demands the rebirth of myth.

It is somehow a blasphemy to compare our time with that of the Homeric epics; it is blasphemy because it was the fantasy of the Nazis to become the new Achaians demolishing an old civilization. However, it is not necessary to compare Hitler with

Achilles when we compare the Mycenian cultural crisis with our own.

It need not be stressed again that, owing to its loss of religious centrality, the present world, at least of the West (although the East surely has not remained untouched), has entered a state of complete disintegration of values, a state in which each single value is in conflict with every other one, trying to dominate them all. The apocalyptic events of the last decades are nothing but the unavoidable outcome of such a dissolution.

Along with these developments, the romantic uneasiness was constantly on the increase. Seeking in an empirical period for some validity, romanticism could only join with an empirical science in a progression which (splitting the world more and more into fragmentary disciplines) increased the hunger of its search. Art became naturalistic, veristic, scientific in its methods, running through the sequences of Impressionism, until at last, in an ultimate despair of expression, it has become expressionistic. If in all these forms it renders the reality of our time, it does so in fact only as anarchy reflecting anarchy.

Thus it is only natural that there came to be a mood of deep distaste for this kind of art, and even for art at all. This distaste is felt neither by the general public which, though sometimes bored, consumes what it is served, nor is it felt by the pseudo-artist who accepts success as a proof of his quality, but it is felt by the few genuine artists, and by those who know that art which does not render the totality of the world is no art. If art can or may exist further, it has to set itself the task of striving for the essential, of becoming a counterbalance to the hypertrophic calamity of the world. And imposing such a task on the arts, this epoch of disintegration imposes on them the style of old age, the style of the essential, the style of the abstract.

The French painters at the turn of the century were the first—significantly guided by technical considerations—who were aware that the whole naturalistic, and unavoidably naturalistic, vocabulary had become obsolete, and that the essential had to be found, even at the price of abstractness. More and more the painter lost interest in the individual fact; the artist's goal was no longer to reproduce the smiling Mrs. X, but (whether or not he achieved it), to strive for the essence of smile. This search led, through increasing sophistications of technique, to the experiments of non-objective art.

Picasso's development is paradigmatic of these processes, all the more so since he achieved in one work a real and perhaps the first full expression of our time: this is "Guernica," a picture so abstract that it could even renounce all color, a picture expressing horror, sorrow, mourning—nothing else, and for this very reason the strongest rebellion against the evil.

Seen from the technical side, abstract art deals with problems very near to those of music, for music is the abstract art *par excellence*. The further the arts move in the direction of abstractism, the closer become the theoretical ties between them: the connec-

28

tion between music and painting is stronger in our time than ever before. And this applies even to poetry and literature; the work of Joyce gains its artistic validity in a very large measure from the musical elements and principles on which it is built.

The striking relationship between the arts on the basis of their common abstractism, their common style of old age, this hallmark of our epoch is the cause of the inner relationship between artists like Picasso, Stravinsky and Joyce. This relationship is not only striking in itself but also by reason of the parallelism through which the style of old age was imposed on these men, even in their rather early years.

Nevertheless, abstractism forms no *Gesamtkunstwerk*—the ideal of the late romantic; the arts remain separate. Literature especially can never become completely abstract and "musicalized": therefore the style of old age relies here much more on another symptomatic attitude, namely on the trend toward myth. It is highly significant that Joyce goes back to the *Odyssey*. And although this return to myth— already anticipated in Wagner—is nowhere so elaborated as in Joyce's work, it is for all that a general attitude of modern literature: the revival of Biblical themes, as, for instance, in the novels of Thomas Mann, is an evidence of the impetuosity with which myth surges to the forefront of poetry. However, this is only a return—a return to myth in its ancient forms (even when they are so modernized as in Joyce), and so far it is not a new myth, not *the* new

myth. Yet, we may assume that at least the first realization of such a new myth is already evident, namely
in Franz Kafka's writings.

In Joyce one may still detect neo-romantic trends,
a concern with the complications of the human soul,
which derives directly from nineteenth-century literature, from Stendhal, and even from Ibsen. Nothing
of this kind can be said about Kafka. Here the personal problem no longer exists, and what seems still
personal is, in the very moment it is uttered, dissolved
in a super-personal atmosphere. The prophecy of
myth is suddenly at hand. And like every true
prophecy it is ethical: for where now are the old
problems of poetry, the problems of love, marriage,
betrayal and jealousy, when murder and rape and
degradation are threatening the human being at every
moment of his life, and nothing remains but sorrow
and mourning? And what painter would still invite
the spectator to rest under the idyllic trees of his
landscape, when the landscapes of this earth have
become exclusively roads of flight and persecution?
Abstractism had attacked the private problems of
men from the technical side, eliminating them from
the realm of art; with Kafka it becomes apparent that
they have lost their ethical validity as well: private
problems have become as distasteful as sordid crimes.
It is the last condemnation of all romanticism, of all
these direct connections between the single private
case and the universe, between the single fact and
the general idea, as it is overemphasized by the
romantic conception.

However, near as this point of view is to that of the French existentialists, Kafka does not belong to them, and his distaste for the private problem, especially in art, is not identical with their *"nausée,"* though like them he knows that the utter isolation in which the single fact is plunged reduces all art and literature to non-existence. For they still remain in the sphere of traditional literature, traditional even when no longer employed for its own sake, but only, as in the existentialist novels and plays, for its value as parable—often approaching legend—to illustrate and concretize their philosophical theories; while Kafka aims in the exactly opposite direction, namely at abstraction, not at concretization—at an untheoretical abstraction to which he was driven exclusively by ethical concerns—and therefore transcends literature. He has reached the point of the Either-Or: either poetry is able to proceed to myth, or it goes bankrupt. Kafka, in his presentiment of the new cosmogony, the new theogony that he had to achieve, struggling with his love for literature, his disgust for literature, feeling the ultimate insufficiency of any artistic approach, decided (as did Tolstoy, faced with a similar decision) to quit the realm of literature, and asked that his work be destroyed; he asked this for the sake of the universe whose new mythical concept had been bestowed upon him.

Man as such is our time's problem; the problems of men are fading away and are even forbidden, morally forbidden. The personal problem of the individual has become a subject of laughter for the gods, and they are right in their lack of pity. The individual is reduced to nothing, but humanity can stand against the gods and even against Fate.

This is the dynamic of the Homeric myth. And as a phenomenon of far-reaching importance, it reappears instinctively in the arts of our time. It is like a foreplan of the new myth which in the future may stand at the religious center of mankind's system of values. Art of itself cannot form the myth, but it points in that direction, because it is expression of the human needs.

Hitler thought to establish the new myth by forbidding the personal problems of men to exist. But his was pseudo-myth, for the real myth lives in the problem of human existence, the problem of man as such. However, if God has to exist, the devil eventually has to serve Him, and it is just the Nazi terror which may still ripen humanity for the ethical theogony in which the new myth will receive its being: if this happens, Fate again will be humanized, and presumably it will be not only human, as was Homer's Force, but also humane, in so far as it is in accord with Europe's Christian tradition. Homer's Force was to have been supplanted by Jehovah's justice, Jehovah's justice by Christ's love. "Through cruelty force confesses its powerlessness to achieve omnipotence."

To show these correspondences seems to have been Rachel Bespaloff's purpose in linking the Homeric epic with Biblical prophecy. In doing so she endows the Homeric work with a new significance for our time—a significance rather Kierkegaardian than existentialist—and it is from here that her interpretation gains a large measure of its essential importance. Were this the only justification of her analysis, this alone would suffice.

H. B.

ON THE ILIAD

To Nicia

Hector

UFFERING and loss have stripped Hector bare; he has nothing left but himself. In the crowd of mediocrities that are Priam's sons, he stands alone, a prince, born to rule. Neither superman, nor demigod, nor godlike, he is a man and among men a prince. He is at ease in a kind of unstudied nobility that permits neither pride in respect to the self nor humbleness in respect to the gods. Loaded as he is with favors, he has much to lose; and there is something in him that sets him above the favors, the natural endowments—his passion for defying destiny. Apollo's protégé, Ilion's protector, defender of a city, a wife, a child, Hector is the guardian of the perishable joys. The zeal for glory exalts but does not blind him; it sustains him when hope has left him.

"For I know well in my entrails and my heart, a day will come when holy Troy will perish." He has learned "to be brave at all times," "to fight in the first ranks of the Trojans." These are his privileges as a prince, which all Andromache's tender urgency cannot make him renounce. And yet he is far from insensible to her plea. It is on Andromache's account, more than on his people's, his father's, his brothers', that the thought of the future tortures him. The very image of the brutal fate that awaits her makes him wish for death. "But as for me, may I be dead, and may the earth have covered me before I hear you cry out or see you dragged away into slavery." Standing there on the threshold of war, Hector clasps with a last look the true goods of life, exposed suddenly to attack, naked as targets. The pain of this leave-taking does not modify his decision which has already been made. "Men will watch in war," and Hector first of all among those who were born in Troy.

Achilles pays for nothing; to Hector everything comes dear. Yet it is not Hector, but Achilles, whose insatiable rancor feeds even on victories, and who is forever "gorging himself with complaints." The man of resentment in the *Iliad* is not the weak man but, on the contrary, the hero who can bend everything to his will. With Hector, the will to greatness never pits itself against the will to happiness. That little bit of true happiness which is more important than anything else, because it coincides with the true meaning of life, will be worth defending even with life itself, to which it has given a measure, a form, a price. Even in defeat, the courage of Hector does not give way before the valor of Achilles, which has been nurtured on discontent and irritable anxiety. But the capacity for happiness, which rewards the efforts of fecund civilizations, puts a curb on the defender's mettle by making him more aware of the enormity of the sacrifice exacted by the gods of war. This capacity, however, does not develop until the appetite for happiness has been stilled, the appetite that drives the aggressor, who is less civilized, on toward his prey and fills his heart with "an infinite power for battle and truceless war."

Death, for Hector, means consigning everything he loves to a life of punishment and torture; flight, on the other hand, is a denial of the thing that transcends him, that "glory" that will some day be the subject of a song and bring Ilion back to life in the centuries to come. Before the walls of Troy, preparing himself to meet Achilles, shaken by premonitions of defeat and by the entreaties of Priam and Hecuba, Hector experiences a kind of ultimate hesitation. Why not keep "peace with dignity" by promising Achilles Helen and half the wealth of Troy? But quickly he gets hold of himself: the war is not in Achilles' hands. Achilles is as deaf to arguments, promises, and human feeling as a hurricane. "Better to meet him at once and have it over with." And now, for the first time perhaps, Hector feels weakness seize him; when he catches sight of his leaping adversary, he is no longer master of his terror. Time after time he has turned the tide of battle, he has taken the measure of Ajax and the very bravest of the Achaians; yet now he, the dauntless, "leaves and takes to flight." Homer wanted him to be a whole man and spared him neither the quaking of terror nor the shame of cowardice. "Ahead flees a brave man, but braver still is he who pursues him at top speed." And this flight, short as it is, has the eternity of a nightmare. "As a man in a dream cannot catch the one he is chasing and as he, in his turn, cannot flee faster than the other pursues, so Achilles that day could not overtake Hector nor could Hector escape him." Homer, here, reaches across history to the very substance of the horror that has neither issue nor redemption. Not around the walls of Troy but in the cosmic womb itself does the ravisher's pursuit prolong endlessly the victim's flight. "And all the gods looked on." Hector makes a last effort, which would have to be called superhuman, did it not pre- cisely define the height and breadth of man's powers: he turns and faces his enemy, having first mastered himself. "I no longer wish to flee you, son of Peleus. . . . It is over. . . . I will have you or you will have me." What he fled from, what he now confronts, is not the "gigantic Achilles," but his own destiny; he meets the appointed hour when he will be sent to pasture in Hades. At least he will not die without a struggle, and not without glory. Dying, he begs Achilles for a last time not to give his body to the dogs. And for a last time his conqueror, drunk with cruelty, is obdurate to his plea. Achilles, at this moment, is aware of not being a man, and admits it:

"There are no covenants between men and lions. . . . It is not permitted that we should love each other, you and I." Agony sets Hector free; he recognizes his mistake and yields himself simultaneously to truth and to death: "Yes, I see what you are. I could never have persuaded you. A heart of iron is in you for sure."

In the absence of God, fate becomes the agent of retribution. Hector has to pay for Patroclus' inglorious death, just as Achilles, later on, will pay for the death of Hector. "Ares is just; he kills those who kill." In the excitement engendered by bloodshed, Hector himself forgets the code of honor. The idea of degrading a fallen enemy is no more repugnant to him than it is to his rival. Both of them, pushing revenge to the point of impiety, desecrate the victim's body so as to kill straight through to the soul. Between the two scenes in which a conquered man's body is outraged, a most rigorous parallelism is kept. "Death and imperious fate" are announced to Hector by Patroclus, and Hector predicts to Achilles his "death at the Scaean gates." War devours differences and disparities, shows no respect for the unique. Call him Achilles or Hector, the conqueror is like all conquerors, and the conquered like all the conquered. Homer does not spare us this sight. But at the same time he sees warlike emulation as the fountainhead of creative effort, as the spring of individual energy and of the manly virtues in the community. Through it the appetite for glory takes hold of individuals and peoples and transforms itself into a love of immortality. Yet, throughout the *Iliad*, the pride of omnipotence is also the thing that invites the reprisals of destiny. Outside all sanctions of the moral order, outside all imperatives of divine origin, the vengeance of the Nemesis of antiquity *makes an act appear guilty in retrospect that at the time of its commission was not considered a sin.* When the Father of the Gods takes out his golden scales to learn fate's decree, the Killer is free to accomplish his sacred mission: he is under the protection of the Immortals. And yet this immunity lasts but an instant; he has hardly fulfilled his allotted role, the force in him is still unspent, when once again he becomes vulnerable.

Force revels only in an abuse that is also self-abuse, in an excess that expends its store. It reveals itself in a kind of supreme leap, a murderous lightning stroke, in which calculation, chance, and power seem to fuse in a single element to defy man's fate. Herein lies the beauty of force, which is nowhere so well shown as in Homer—with the exception, possibly, of the Bible, which glorifies it in God alone. When Homer celebrates the beauty of his warriors, he does not intend to stylize or idealize them; Achilles and Hector are beautiful because force is beautiful, and because the beauty of omnipotence, converted into the omnipotence of beauty, can make man acquiesce utterly in his own destruction, can exact from him that flat submission that delivers him over to force, prostrate in the act of worship. Thus, in the *Iliad*, force appears as both the supreme reality and the supreme illusion of life. Force, for Homer, is divine insofar as it represents a superabundance of life that flashes out in the contempt for death and the ecstasy of self-sacrifice; it is detestable insofar as it contains a fatality that transforms it into inertia, a blind drive that is always pushing it on to the very end of its course, on to its own abolition and the obliteration of the very values it engendered. To illustrate the illusion of omnipotence, Homer chooses not, as one might expect, Achilles or Ajax, but the prince of wisdom himself. A fleeting triumph befuddles Hector; he loses the power of reflection, the sense of proportion; he is no longer aware of the existence of obstacles. When Polydamas counsels prudence, he angrily rejects his advice and threatens him with death for holding defeatist ideas. But Polydamas is surely right to accuse Hector of being always the same in council and in war, unable to brook contradiction: "There is only one thing that pleases you, the perpetual increase of your authority." In Homer, the hero himself, even Achilles, cannot set himself above the human plane. Hector has nothing, courage, nobility, or reason, that is not bent and sullied by war, nothing except that self-respect that makes him human, comes to his rescue at the end, steadies him before the inevitable, and brings him his clearest vision in the instant of death.

Hector, then, has but this way to glory, "the tale of which will pass on to men yet to come." And for Homer's warrior, glory is not some vain illusion or empty boast; it is the same thing that Christians saw in the Redemption, a promise of immortality outside and beyond history, in the supreme detachment of poetry. Achilles ravens on Hector's remains. Every day, starting at dawn, he devotes himself to his lust for reprisal; three times in succession he drags his unfortunate rival's body around the tomb of Patroclus and then leaves it there, stretched out in the dust. His insatiable spleen vents itself both on Patroclus' murderer and on that defeated being, now out of his reach, who reminds him of the futility of victory and the approach of his own death. The gods, however, who took everything else that belonged to Hector, have neither the power nor the wish to deprive him of the beauty that outlives force. Stretched out prone in the dirt, he remains beautiful: "Apollo spares his body all pollution . . . Aphrodite, night and day, keeps the dogs from him." And, intact thus in his young warrior's beauty, he will be given back to Priam. On this point Hermes reassures the old man, who questions his guide anxiously before approaching Achilles: "You would marvel yourself if you were to come and see how dewy he lies there, the blood around him washed away, without a sign of pollution, and all his wounds closed. So the blessed gods care for your son, even in death, for he was dear to their hearts."

Not the wrath of Achilles, but the duel between Achilles and Hector, the tragic confrontation of the revenge-hero and the resistance-hero, is what forms the *Iliad's* true center and governs its unity and its development. Despite the gods, despite necessity, there is enough freedom here to leave both the reader and Zeus, the divine watcher, in a state of suspense. The changing rhythm of the battle pits the defenders' valor against the invaders' fury in a constantly shifting relation which makes every contestant uncertain of the future. This fluctuation of fortune, however, does not stop the Achaians and the Trojans from calculating, with a kind of muffled lucidity, their respective chances in the "indefinite series of duels" whose ensemble is the Trojan War. Whatever befalls them, the petty pirate kings never lose faith in their own invincibility; Ilion's princes, on the contrary, cannot, even on the brink of victory, shake off a premonition of defeat. By the time Hector dares to face Achilles without despairing of victory, he has already used up the better part of his strength in winning a prior victory over himself. Achilles' mission is to renew, amid these scenes of devastation, the sources and resources of vital energy; Hector's is to preserve, by the gift of himself, the sacred trust whose maintenance assures to life its profound continuity. But these roles, these functions, do not reveal themselves in their true light until the crucial moment of combat when Hector's courage matures into a sovereign act of self-mastery and Achilles' anger mounts into murderous ecstasy. In this light the destinies of the two men appear to be permanently interlocked in struggle, death, and immortality. Where history showed us only ramparts and frontiers, poetry discovered a mysterious predestination that makes two adversaries, whose meeting is inexorable, worthy of each other. And Homer asks no quarter, save from poetry, which repossesses beauty from death and wrests from it the secret of justice that history cannot fathom. To the darkened world poetry alone restores pride, eclipsed by the arrogance of the victors and the silence of the vanquished. Others may blame Zeus and marvel that he permits "the good to be ranked with the bad, those whose souls turn toward justice with those who are given over to violence."[1] With Homer there is no marvelling or blaming, and no answer is expected. Who is good in the *Iliad?* Who is bad? Such distinctions do not exist; there are only men suffering, warriors fighting, some winning, some losing. The passion for justice emerges only in mourning for justice, in the dumb avowal of silence. To condemn force, or absolve it, would be to condemn, or absolve, life itself. And life in the *Iliad* (as in the Bible or in *War and Peace*) is essentially the thing that does not permit itself to be assessed, or measured, or condemned, or justified, at least not by the living. Any estimate of life must be confined to an awareness of its inexpressibility. This pliable wisdom, consubstantial with existence itself, has very little in common with the parade drills of Stoicism.

Sprung out of bitterness, the philosophy of the *Iliad* excludes resentment. It antedates the divorce between nature and existence. Here the Whole is no

[1] Compare this text from Theognis with the words of Habakkuk: "Thine eyes are too pure to see evil. And Thou canst not look at iniquity. Why shouldst Thou look with favor on the false-hearted and be silent when the wicked man devours one juster than himself?"

collection of broken pieces put back together with indifferent success by reason; on the contrary, it is the active principle of interpenetration of all the elements that make it up. The inevitable slowly unfolds, and its theatre is the heart of man, and, at the same time, the Cosmos. Against the eternal blindness of history is set the creative lucidity of the poet fashioning for future generations heroes more godlike than the gods, and more human than men.

Thetis and Achilles

N O WRITER has ever achieved such lucid tenderness and delicate precision as Homer when he speaks of the bond between Thetis and Achilles. This man of passion, driven from restless boredom to frenzied action, is son to a goddess, to a light-footed Nereid whose grace enfolds him in calm. From the depths of that submarine retreat where she dwells with her old father, Thetis keeps watch over her son, and her vigilance never sleeps. "From the deep of marine abysses," or from the peaks of Olympus, she is always darting to his side with exhortations and soothing words. The anxious love that has taught her the lesson of human distress has also taught her to despise her immortal status. Beside the earth-bound Achilles, whom force has made half-god, and violence half-beast, Thetis herself becomes earthly, the better to suffer, the better to feel death's threat.

How winning she is when she appeals to Zeus! Wrapped in her dark-blue mantle ("there is no blacker garment"), she cleaves the turbid deep. The gods love Thetis and receive her with favor. Athena yields her the place of honor, next to Zeus the Father. Hephæstus hurries off to gratify her every wish. But she flees the Olympians. Forever lamenting her doomed son, "forever ready to fly, night and day, to his side," she dreads the gods' insouciance which she sees as an insult to her "unforgettable grief"; their company is distasteful to her. Zeus, after all, outraged the goddess in her by delivering her to Peleus, whose bitter old age weighs heavy on her immortal youth. She does not forget the injury, and she remains much less the wife of Peleus than the Sea's daughter and Achilles' mother. Her dual nature, human and divine, fulfills itself in this love which bitterness preserves from corruption. And the double thread that binds her to the elements, on the one hand, and to human passions, on the other, brings existence and fable together in her person.

She retains all the freshness of a young mother leaning over the baby that isolates her from the world. How well this Nereid knows her son, though she sits hidden in her wave-palace; what perspicacity her love gains from its obsession with the fate that will take Achilles away from her! Yet she does not, for all her fears, try to deflect Achilles from his course, once he has made up his mind to revenge himself on the Trojans. "Do not try," he says to her, "however much you love me, to keep me far from battle." And Thetis is not such a fool as to break into idle lamentations. She is satisfied if she can arouse Achilles from his brooding resentment and set him a nobler aim than vengeance. "It is not wrong to save our dear ones, when they have come to the end of their powers, from death's abyss." She does not scold him; she busies herself in his behalf and pleads his cause with Zeus. She only asks her son to wait until he has got the new arms that Hephæstus, at her request, will make for him. And in the end, it is to Thetis that Zeus turns to get this madman to come to his senses and restore Hector's remains to Priam. On this mission, she is all tenderness and consolation. "She sits down beside him and caresses him with her hand and speaks to him, calling him by all his names." Achilles submits to the gods' command, conveyed to him by his mother: the untamable is tamed; in obedience he finds for a moment the serenity that is always eluding him.

In the same degree that Hector's respect for his "worthy mother," the tiresome and solemn Hecuba, is conventional, Achilles' attachment to Thetis is true, spontaneous, and ardent. Hector has Andromache. Achilles has only a collection of beautiful captives who weep tractably at his command, sobbing in chorus, "seemingly for Patroclus but in reality for their own fate." When the ponderous Agamemnon robs him of Briseis, his "rightful share," it is his self-love more than his love that is injured. Outside of

Patroclus, the only being that Achilles is capable of affection for is Thetis of the fair tresses, the mother, immortal and young. At her side he relaxes in his need for protection and consolation. Thetis herself never plays the mother of the conquering hero; she remains the tortured mother of a son in agony. Her presence restores Achilles to a juster sense of human proportion; she saves him from dissolving into myth. In her presence, bombast and stress disappear: from the hero, the embodiment of force, comes only a cry of frustration. She nurtured her son "like a young plant at the side of a vineyard," but she did not succeed in making him immortal. Through this failure he becomes accessible to us. His destiny, crueller perhaps than Hector's, nails him to misfortune. Committed to injustice, Achilles has no choice but to inflict it or undergo it himself.

In the last analysis, it is not through action that Homer reveals man's profoundest nature but rather through man's ways of loving and choosing his love. For Hector, love is the forgetfulness of self. For Achilles, self is at the center of love. What he adores in Patroclus[1] is his own reflection, purified—in Thetis, the sacred origin of his line. In the thick of war and hate intimacy flowers unexpectedly, deriving strength and purity from the dangers that surround it. The love of Hector and Andromache, the affection of Thetis and Achilles brings it close to perfection. Young Lycaon's murderer can strip himself of the

[1] Patroclus is the only character in the *Iliad* whose personality remains dim.

last thread of pity and humanity; he remains Thetis' son. From her he inherits a grace even in the midst of violence, a generosity that is quick and unpremeditated. There is no baseness in Achilles; force in its purity rejects treachery and cunning; it kills, it does not degrade, nor does it degrade itself in self-satisfaction. For Achilles, his dual nature, half-human, half-divine, is mainly a source of jars and discords. As a god, he envies the gods their omnipotence and immortality; as a man, he envies the beasts their ferocity, and says he would like to tear his victims' bodies to pieces and eat them raw. He spends himself without reckoning, in a rapture of aggressiveness. Surrounded by his Myrmidons, more like a chief than a king, Achilles cares but little for his kingdom. Destiny, he knows, can "carry him off to death," by two quite different routes. He has chosen the steep road that ends on the edge of the abyss. He will sacrifice home-coming, reunion with his father and his son, for the pleasure of massacring the Trojans, avenging Patroclus, and watching both friends and foes quake at the sight of him.

With surprising objectivity, Homer shows us the limits of force in the very apotheosis of the force-hero. Through cruelty force confesses its powerlessness to achieve omnipotence. When Achilles falls upon Lycaon, shouting "death to all," and makes fun of the child who is pleading with him, he lays bare the eternal resentment felt by the will to power when something gets in the way of its indefinite expansion. We see weakness dawning at the very height of force. Unable to admit that total destruction is impossible, the conqueror can only reply to the mute defiance of his defenceless adversary with an ever-growing violence. Achilles will never get the best of the thing he kills: Lycaon's youth will rise again and Priam's wisdom and Ilion's beauty. And, yet, the royal ease of Achilles, when he does not reach the limits of his power, remains a true image of grandeur. Achilles' heroism is not so breath-taking as his discontent, his marvellous ingratitude. The sport of war, the joys of pillage, the luxury of rage, "when it swells in a human breast, sweeter than honey on a human tongue," the glitter of empty triumphs and mad enterprises—all these things are Achilles. Without Achilles, men would have peace; without Achilles, they would sleep on, frozen with boredom, till the planet itself grew cold.

Helen

O F ALL the figures in the poem she is the severest, the most austere. Shrouded in her long white veils, Helen walks across the *Iliad* like a penitent; misfortune and beauty are consummate in her and lend majesty to her step. For this royal recluse freedom does not exist; the very slave who numbers the days of oppression on some calendar of hope is freer than she. What has Helen to hope for? Nothing short of the death of the Immortals would restore her freedom, since it is the gods, not her fellow men, who have dared to put her in bondage. Her fate does not depend on the outcome of the war; Paris or Menelaus may get her, but for her nothing can really change. She is the prisoner of the passions her beauty excited, and her passivity is, so to speak, their underside.

Aphrodite rules her despotically; the goddess commands and Helen bows, whatever her private repugnance. Pleasure is extorted from her; this merely makes her humiliation the more cruel. Her only resource is to turn against herself a wrath too weak to spite the gods. She seems to live in horror of herself. "Why did I not die before?" is the lament that keeps rising to her lips. Homer is as implacable toward Helen as Tolstoy is toward Anna. Both women have run away from home thinking that they could abolish the past and capture the future in some unchanging essence of love. They awake in exile and feel nothing but a dull disgust for the shrivelled ecstasy that has outlived their hope. The promise of freedom has been sloughed off in servitude; love does not obey the rules of love but yields to some more ancient and ruder law. Beauty and death have become neighbors and from their alliance springs a necessity akin to that of force. When Helen and Anna come to and face their deteriorated dream, they can blame only themselves for having been the dupes of harsh Aphrodite. Everything they squandered comes back on them; everything they touch turns to dust or stone. In driving his heroine to suicide, Tolstoy goes beyond Christianity and rejoins Homer and the tragic poets. To them the hero's flaw is indistinguishable from the misery that arises from it. The sufferer bears it; he pays for it, but he cannot redeem it any more than he can live his life over. Clytemnestra, Orestes and Oedipus are their crimes; they have no existence outside them. Later on, the philosophers, heirs of

Odysseus, introduce the Trojan horse of dialectic
into the realm of tragedy. Error takes the place of
the tragic fault, and the responsibility for it rests with
the individual alone. With Homer, punishment and
expiation have the opposite effect; far from fixing
responsibility, they dissolve it in the vast sea of human
suffering and the diffuse guilt of the life-process itself.
A flaw in a defective universe is not quite the same
thing as a sin; remorse and grace have not yet made
their appearance. But it is nonetheless true that this
Greek idea of a diffuse guilt represents for Homer and
the tragic poets the equivalent of the Christian idea of
original sin. Fed on the same reality, charged with
the same weight of experience, it contains the same
appraisal of existence. It too acknowledges a fall, but
a fall that has no date and has been preceded by no
state of innocence and will be followed by no redemption; the fall, here, is a continuous one as the
life-process itself which heads forever downward
into death and the absurd. In proclaiming the innocence of Becoming, Nietzsche is as far from the
ancients as he is from Christianity. Where Nietzsche
wants to justify, Homer simply contemplates, and
the only sound that he lets ring through his lines is
the plaint of the hero. If the final responsibility for
the tragic guilt rests on the mischievous gods, this
does not mean that guilt is nonexistent. On the contrary, there is not a page in the *Iliad* that does not
emphasize its irreducible character. So fully does
Helen assume it that she does not even permit herself the comfort of self-defense. In Helen, purity and

guilt mingle confusedly as they do in the vast heart of the warrior herd spread out on the plain at her feet.

Thus Helen, at Ilion, drags her ill luck along with a kind of somber humility that still makes no truce with the gods.[1] But is it really Aphrodite? Is it not rather the Asiatic Astarte who has trapped her? In a certain way, Helen's destiny prefigures that of Greece which, from the Trojan War to Alexander's conquests, was alternately submitting to and repelling the tremendous attraction of the Orient. What the exile misses in Paris' high dwelling is not the blond Achaian, arrogant Menelaus, son of a wild race of Northern barbarians, but the rude, pure homeland—the familiar city, the child she used to fondle.

How tired she gets of the soft, weak ways of Aphrodite's protégé; he is a humiliation and a wound to her. "If the gods have decreed these evils for us, why could not I have had a husband who was capable of a feeling of revolt?" Here in hostile Troy, where boredom makes her despondent, Helen has no one to cling to but Hector, the least oriental of Priam's sons, the most manly, the most Greek. There is a feeling of tenderness between them. Helen's presence is odious to everyone, and Hector is her only defender from the hatred she excites. Nobody can forgive the stranger for being the embodiment of the fatality that pursues the city. Innocent though she is, Helen feels the weight of these rebukes; she even

---

[1] And possibly this royal humility, in Helen and Œdipus, is what distinguishes the antique style from the Christian.

seems to invite them, as though courting a just
punishment for a crime she did not commit. She is
all the more grateful, therefore, to the one person
who shows her compassion without importuning her
with lust. When Hector comes to scold Paris, Helen
is worried about the dangers that threaten her
brother-in-law. He is the only one to whom she
speaks gently: "Meanwhile, come in, brother, and
take this seat. Care assails your heart more than any-
one else's, and that because of me, bitch that I am,
and the folly of Alexander. Zeus has given us a hard
lot, that later on we may be the subject of a song
for men to come." These words weave a complicity
between Hector and Helen that is something more
than fraternal. With an unequalled insight, Homer
hears in their talk an accent of intimacy which is
attuned to the truth of human relationships. This
affection, on Helen's part at least, shields a deeper
feeling, which Homer, listening, does not betray.

The exile's lament is the last to echo over Hector's
remains; it bathes the end of the *Iliad* in the pure,
desolate light of compassion. "This is now the twentieth year from the time I came away and left my
native land; yet I have never heard a bad or a harsh
word from you. So I weep for you and for my
unhappy self too, with grief at heart. I have nobody
else now in wide Troy to be kind or gentle to me;
everybody shudders away from me." This, however,
is not the moan of some humiliated creature at the
mercy of her tormentors; it is the grief of a mortal
at the mercy of gods who have laden her with

dazzling graces, the better to balk her of the joy these gifts seemed to promise. No matter who wins in the end, Helen, unlike Andromache and the Trojan princesses, does not have to fear a life of slavery and forced labor "under the eyes of a harsh master." After twenty years, she is still the stake the war is being fought for, and the reward the winner will carry off. In the depths of her wretchedness, Helen still wears an air of majesty that keeps the world at a distance and flouts old age and death. The most beautiful of women seemed born for a radiant destiny; everything pointed that way; everything appeared to contribute to it. But, as it turns out, the gods only chose her to work misfortune on herself and on the two nations. Beauty is not a promise of happiness here; it is a burden and a curse. At the same time, it isolates and elevates; it has something preservative in it that wards off outrage and shame. Hence its sacred character—to use the word in its original, ambiguous sense—on the one hand, life-giving, exalting; on the other, accursed and dread. The Helen the two armies are contending for will never be Paris' any more than she has been Menelaus'; the Trojans cannot own her any more than the Greeks could. Beauty, captured, remains elusive. It deserts alike those who beget, or contemplate, or desire it. Homer endows it with the inexorability of force or fate. Like force, it subjugates and destroys —exalts and releases. It is not by some chance, arising out of her life's vicissitudes, that Helen has come to be the cause of the war and its stake; a deeper

necessity has brought her there to join the appari-
tion of beauty with the unleashing of rage. Beside
the warriors and above them, Helen is the calm and
the bitterness that spring up in the thick of battle,
casting their cool shadow over victories and defeats
alike, over the living and the thousands of dead. For,
if force degrades itself in the insignificance of Becoming (one arrow from Paris' bow puts an end to the
might of Achilles), beauty alone transcends all con-
tingencies, including those that brought it to flower.
The origins of Leda's daughter are lost in fable, her
end in legend. In immortal appearance the world of
Being is maintained and protected.

Homer carefully abstains from the description of
beauty, as though this might constitute a forbidden
anticipation of bliss. The shade of Helen's eyes, of
Thetis' tresses, the line of Andromache's shoulders
—these details are kept from us. No singularity, no
particularity is brought to our notice; yet we see
these women; we would recognize them. One
wonders by what impalpable means Homer manages
to give us such a sense of the plastic reality of his
characters. Incorruptible, Helen's beauty passes from
life into the poem, from flesh into marble, its pulse
still throbbing. The statue's mouth utters a human
cry, and from the empty eyes gush "tender tears."
When Helen climbs the ramparts of Troy to watch
the fight between Paris and Menelaus, one can almost
feel the loftiness of her step. By the Scaean gates, the
Trojan elders are holding council. At the sight of her,
"the good orators" fall silent, struck to the heart.

They cannot help finding her beautiful. And this beauty frightens them like a bad omen, a warning of death. "She has terribly the look, close-up, of the immortal goddesses. . . . But even so, whatever she may be, let her set sail and go away. Let her not be left here to be a scourge to us and our sons hereafter." Here—and this is unusual—the poet himself, speaking through Priam, lifts his voice to exonerate beauty and proclaim it innocent of man's misfortunes. "I do not blame you. I blame the gods, who launched this Achaian war, full of tears, upon me." The real culprits, and the only ones, are the gods, who live "exempt from care," while men are consumed with sorrow. The curse which turns beauty into destructive fatality does not originate in the human heart. The diffuse guilt of Becoming pools into a single sin, the one sin condemned and explicitly stigmatized by Homer: the happy carelessness of the Immortals.

There follows a scene of starry serenity in which the human accent, however, is still audible. Priam asks Helen to tell him the names of the most famous of the Achaian warriors that he can see in the enemy camp. The battlefield is quiet; a few steps away from each other, the two armies stand face to face awaiting the single combat that will decide the outcome of the war. Here, at the very peak of the *Iliad*, is one of those pauses, those moments of contemplation, when the spell of Becoming is broken, and the world of action, with all its fury, dips into peace. The plain where the warrior herd was raging is no more than a tranquil mirage to Helen and the old king.

No doubt this is where Nietzsche listened to the dialogue between Beauty and Wisdom, set above life but very close to it. "Pushed, pressed, constrained, tracked down by torment," come at length to the place where, around him, everything "turned strange and solitary," he had a vision of Helen (or Ariadne), high and inaccessible against the blue sky.

Meanwhile Helen stands helplessly watching the men who are going to do battle for her. She is there still, since nations that brave each other for markets, for raw materials, rich lands, and their treasures, are fighting, first and forever, for Helen.

The Comedy of the Gods

THE *Iliad* has its share of the comic spirit. It even has humor: the Olympians supply it. Zeus's court plays much the same role that worldly society and Alexander's satellites play in *War and Peace*. The absolute futility of beings who are exempted by fortune from the common lot achieves, in the Immortals, a kind of showy, decorative stateliness. The gods of the *Iliad* and the worldlings of *War and Peace* have that want of seriousness (and by *seriousness* I do not mean *heaviness*) that for Homer, as for Tolstoy, is the distinguishing mark of the subhuman; this is what makes them such exquisite comic figures. Everything that happens has been caused by them, but they take no responsibility, whereas the epic heroes take total responsibility even for that which they have not caused. The gods' irresponsibility begins at home; they are not responsible for themselves. Where the free individual is not asserting himself against Fate, responsibility has nothing to grasp. Anger spills out in a burst of laughter that sanctions the triumph of incoherence. Thus the gods elude moral classifications; both innocence and sin are beyond them. *Agents provocateurs*, smart propagandists, heated partisans, these non-belligerents do not mind the smell of carnage or the clash of tragic passions. Condemned to a permanent security, they would die of boredom without intrigues and war. "You are cruel and mischievous, you gods," cries Apollo, who does not like them.

This irreverence encroaches not at all on Homer's respect for piety. The pact that binds the city to its divine protector hallows a tradition in which a style of life is embodied. The one thing that is unassailable, that is essential to the heart of man, is tradition, which extorts from the life-process the secret of continuity. It is the only thing that can make man's shackles pleasant to him and that can even invest these bonds with certain magical properties. The god's statue may topple from the pedestal, but the sacred base remains. The heroes of the *Iliad* rail against "Kronos' hateful son," whenever they have reason to complain of him, but there is no sacrilege in it, and Zeus himself does not take exception to these carryings-on. If the elders of the city can blame the gods, whom, after all, they have admitted to their hearths, their councils, their wars, it is because the gods are in good health, receive

74

rich oblations, and are not merely vegetating in the icy respect of a lifeless cult.

For what the Greek, in all piety, asks of his gods, is not love but good will—the consecration of human effort that has reached harmony through the sufferings of excess and the negations of the extreme. If love is totally absent from the relations between men and gods, friendship sometimes replaces it. There is the friendship of Hector and Apollo which has the mutual confidence and esteem, the familiarity and the sense of distance, the joy of give-and-take, that will be seen later in the attachment that a Socrates and a Plato were able to inspire in their disciples. Apollo the Preserver, Hector's friend, nearer to men than to the Immortals, and yet more godlike than these turbulent gods, is really Homer's teacher. He feels pity for men to whom the Parcae "have given a heart apt for suffering." But, as a rule, men and Immortals in the *Iliad* have little in common beyond the ties of interest and expediency that connect the sheltered world of the court and important people with the exposed world of war and fighting men.

The quarrels and reconciliations of Zeus and Hera, the seduction scene in which, armed with Aphrodite's magic ribbon, she manages to make a fool of her husband, the scene where Zeus discovers his wife's trick as he wakes up and threatens to push her off the heights of Olympus and let her hang suspended in the ether, all these really belong to musical comedy. But here, again, truth to human experience somehow moves this marital farce to a plane of more substantial reality. There is Hera with her big stupid eyes, her obstinacy more brutish than evil, and the real genius she shows while subjecting Zeus to a successful "war of nerves," from which she always comes off with the honors. There is Aphrodite, all smiles and whims, enchanting and futile in her weakness, yet not so defenseless as she seems. There is Pallas Athena, a warrior with a man's muscles, expert and treacherous, who can send Ares rolling to the ground with the force of a single blow, who knows how to harbor a grudge and let rancor steep within her until her revenge is brewed. These are the three goddesses involved in the judgment of Paris, and each in her own way reveals the other side of the eternal feminine whose tragic purity is embodied in Andromache, Helen, and Thetis.

Zeus is the only one among the Olympians to have a more complex life. He plays his part in the farce down to the last thunderclap, but this does not prevent him from enjoying the spectacle. The rout of the Trojans certainly grieves him; still, as he says, he wants to keep his seat in the fold of Olympus: "to watch them will charm my heart." After a vain attempt to impose neutrality on the Immortals (whose sole concern is to violate it), Zeus lets them intervene in the conflict. Immediately, they plunge in, and the Father of the Gods laughs to see them hurling each other about while "the vast earth grumbles," and "the immense heaven blows the horn of battle around them." Athena knocks Ares on the head with an enormous rock; Hera pounds noisy

76

Artemis nearly to pieces; and Achilles takes advantage of the uproar to slaughter Trojans as fast as he can. "The flames of a burning city mount to the vast heaven." This vision is just what Zeus likes. There is nothing of the judge in this watcher-god. A demanding spectator, he accepts the law of tragedy that allows the best and the most noble to perish in order to renew the creativeness of life through sacrifice. When his turbulent crew gets too much for him, he sails off across space in his chariot, till he gets to Mount Ida of the thousand springs. On this peak, "alone in the pride of his glory," he contemplates the city of the Trojans and the Achaian fleet.

The disabused skepticism of Kronos' son is like a strange portent of Ecclesiastes. Zeus is well aware that the gods can die, and he bows before the great blind divinity who governs mortals and Immortals alike. His eye marks the beam that registers the weight of defeat on the golden scales of fatality, and he lets the irreparable have its way. He has preferences, but he does not defend them: will he not abandon Ilion, which is under his special protection, to the furies of Hera? And Hector to the blows of Achilles? Unlike the God of Israel, he does not intervene with punishment or help, revenge or redemption. The indifferent distributor of good and evil, Zeus confines himself to giving the actor the scenario of the drama he has to play in: "Two jars are planted in Zeus's garden, containing the gifts he gives, the bad in one, the good in the other." It is up to man to extract what he can from this mixture.

Zeus the watcher is not, like God the creator, a force set above force, a power of will that can dominate the will to power. Force in him is only a decorative semblance, the symbol of a reality that he represents but does not in any way embody. For Homer, force is more divine in man than in nature. And he only glorifies it in its limited and finite aspect as perishable energy thàt culminates in courage. Inseparable from the perfect body it prompts to action, this energy shares in the eternal play of cosmic forces from which it does not basically differ. The overflowing of the Scamander has the rhythm of human anger; the flight of the hero before the angry river-god retraces the terrible course of myriads of animal stampedes. If Achilles here is merely a part of nature, all of nature echoes the plight of existence, flung into the torrent of phenomena. Endowed with divine and human attributes, nature is far from being that great Whole into which man dissolves in blissful annihilation. On the contrary, nature participates in the struggles of men; heaven and earth, rivers and mountains, take an interest in the conflict.[1]

Zeus alone stays outside of it. He does not knock history into shape with the hammer blows of the God of Israel. For him, history is a show that neither

---

[1] Not the least beautiful passage in the *Iliad* is the one where the Scamander, rising against Achilles, vents its rage. The powerful god, wanting to protect the Trojans from misfortune, falls on Peleus' son "with its black crest." Achilles flees, leaps up, hangs on to the trees on the bank, misses his footing, leaps higher; the inflexible hero knows fear and trembling and hatred of the inexorable. Besieged, encircled, he implores Zeus like a frightened child.

knows divine justice nor asks for it. He will not outlive its pageant. But his serene look, dominating from on high consequences still distant, prevents the Trojan War from being a mere bloody fracas. The passionate interest of the divine spectator conveys to the flux of events its metaphysical meaning. What does it matter if the gods perish with the heroes? The poet's verses, which alone are immortal, will recite the childlike grief of Achilles, Hector's regrets, and the tears of Andromache.

Nietzsche is wrong when he says that Homer is the poet of apotheoses. What he exalts and sanctifies is not the triumph of victorious force but man's energy in misfortune, the dead warrior's beauty, the glory of the sacrificed hero, the song of the poet in times to come—whatever defies fatality and rises superior to it, even in defeat. In this respect, Homer's eternity, which centers around the will of the individual, is opposed to Tolstoy's eternity, in which the split of individuation has been abolished. Going beyond Christianity, the demiurge of Yasnaia Polyana carries us toward Asia, toward India, the home of contemplatives and saints, while the Ionian poet, through paganism, steers us toward the promontories of the Christian Occident.

Troy and Moscow

HOMER and Tolstoy have in common a virile love of war and a virile horror of it. They are neither pacifist nor bellicist. They have no illusions about war and they present it as it really is, in its continual oscillation between boisterous animal spirits that break out in spurts of aggressiveness and the detachment of sacrifice in which the return to the One is consummated. It is hopeless to look in the *Iliad* for a condemnation of war as such. People make war, they put up with it, they curse it, they even praise it in songs and verses, but it is not to be judged any more than destiny is. Silence is the only answer, silence and that disabused, dispassionate look which the dying Hector casts on Achilles, or which Prince Andrey seems to direct toward that indefinite region beyond his own death. For the young men who will replace them and are anxious to get into the game, war still has its power of seduction. "Already my fury is rising and I feel my two feet spring under me." The irreparable has the curious property of inducing forgetfulness by paralyzing the imagination and the memory, which retain no trace of its horrors. Yet while the imagination is overpowered by war, it is at the same time stimulated by a brutal shift of lighting that casts the elemental substance of life into relief. War, in the epic, appears first of all as a kind of prolonged spasm related to the rhythms of anger that are always ravaging nature, the great cosmic upheavals. The imagery of the *Iliad* keeps evoking the savage brotherhood between man and the elements. "He tumbled, as an oak tree tumbles, or a poplar, or a slender pine tree that carpenters with freshly ground axes lay low on a mountaintop to make a ship's keel. Even so he lies, measuring his length on the earth, before his horses and chariot, moaning and clawing at the bloody dust." The vast hubbub of battles resounds to heaven like the din of the elements: "Neither does the sea's wave pounding the land cry as loud when on all sides it rises at the breath of cruel Boreas, nor the blazing fire that flares up in a mountain gorge and kindles the whole forest . . . so mighty was the voice of the Trojans and of the Achaians when, with horrible cries, they hurled themselves the one against the other." But above the tumult, above the fallen warrior waiting "with heavy arm and death before his eyes," for his conqueror to finish him off, opens out the same eternal sky on which Prince Andrey gazed, lying between heaven and time. War itself, then, appears as the way to unity through the flux of Becoming that undoes and remakes worlds, souls and gods. To the life it is forever consuming, it lends a supreme importance. Precisely because war takes everything away from us, the All, whose reality is suddenly forced on us by the tragic vulnerability of our particular existences, becomes inestimable. Anything destined for destruction and ignorant of its danger, or hoping to escape—the simple life, the peace of Andromache giving wheat to Hector's horses, the anxious happiness of Natasha before Andrey goes away—is lit up with tenderness. The All, in these two epics, is more than a backdrop: it is the One—actor and unseen manager of the drama in which men and gods struggle, hopelessly interlocked.

It is impossible to speak of an Homeric world or a Tolstoyan world in the sense that one can speak of a Dantesque world, a Balzacian or Dostoievskian world. Tolstoy's universe, like Homer's is what our own is from moment to moment. We don't step into it; we are there. "As for myself, I find it difficult to tell all; I am not a God." This modest statement in the *Iliad* might have been taken up by Tolstoy on his own. Neither writer finds it necessary to tell all to make the All reveal itself. They are the only ones (Shakespeare excepted) who are capable of those planetary pauses, those musical rests, over an event where history appears in its perpetual flight beyond human ends, in its creative incompleteness. Hector will never see the annihilation of his city's invaders, nor Prince Andrey the reflux of the Napoleonic conquest. For the pagan, there remains the eternity of glory; for the Christian, the eternity of faith. Rooted in this passion for eternity, the love of country never shows itself fully except in the test of war. Faced with this ultimate threat, man understands that his attachment to the country which willingly, or unwillingly, he has made the center of his world, the dwelling place of his gods, and his reason for life or death, is no pious and comfortable feeling, but a grim demand imposed on his whole being. On the eve of Borodino, Prince Andrey, still smarting from the wounds of his broken engagement and his disappointed ambitions, is overwhelmed by a passion more stubborn than love or glory—that of reconquering one's humiliated fatherland. In the same way, during the perilous attack on the wall that protects the Achaian ships, Hector, as he reassembles the Trojans and the Allies for the assault, weighs the force that each individual has in reserve for the defense of his "goods": an earth and a sky, loved ones, things long cherished that have dissolved into the very substance of life. "One omen is best, to fight for one's country," he tells Polydamas. Obliged to be strong or perish, man invents a new way of loving life, a more obstinate one. It took the trials of imprisonment to make Pierre Bezhukhov remember the primary truth that his illusions and yearnings hid from him. Nothing, he sees, is terrible in life because the whole of life is terrible. There is no balance, weight or measure with which to calculate human sufferings. Even Achilles, taker of cities, at the peak of his triumph cannot make out whether oppressing old Priam makes him feel victorious or despairing. In Homer and Tolstoy these great common truths are disclosed to man only when he is alone: they are the revelation made by solitude in the thick of collective action. The necessity imposed on the individual by the threat of slavery or annihilation forces him to endure these truths, but it does not dissolve his personality in the anonymous mass; it denudes him, but at the same time it exalts him. Pierre, Andrey, Hector, and Achilles are never more themselves than when they are on the verge of being nothing. The cities too—burned-out Moscow, empty as a deserted beehive, Ilion threatened in its opulence, soon to be dethroned and dismembered—have individual lives; they have a soul, a fate, a sanctity all their own. Holy Troy, Moscow, holy city, these are the epic's real centers of gravity. They are the geographical point where the threads of events crisscross, and the metaphysical place where the religious transformation of fact into sacred fiction is accomplished. The city may be burned to the ground, not a stone of its buildings left standing, but it survives in the epic as a living witness to the real or imaginary lives it supported, to the real or legendary struggles of which it was the stake.

Neither Homer nor Tolstoy makes any attempt to extenuate the scandal of fruitless suffering; nor do they try to escape from it into the idea of individual survival.[1] They make no appeal from life except to life itself. In their scale of vision the stern affirmation of life as it is, whether viewed in its entirety or in the detail of single destinies, implies the rejection of a First Cause. If Homer exalts individual greatness and delights in it, while Tolstoy chastises and humbles it, he nevertheless does not give it immunity from death. Even Achilles, the man of immoderation, "has, like other men, a skin the bronze point can gash, a life like our own." Homer has not made him invulnerable. No moment passes in which solitude does not touch the hero, reminding him of a time when the spell of war will be broken even for him. When Prince Andrey penetrates to this region, nothing he loved—women, country, glory—goes with him. And when "red death and imperious fate make themselves at home in the eyes of the fallen warrior," nothing remains to him of what had been his pride and his joy. Consciousness is not equipped with wings that would let it soar beyond death and grasp eternity outside time. Life here does not take the form of a continuous evolution from birth to death; rather, it is like a yawning stretch of time with death at the center. For Homer, as for Tolstoy, death keeps its sting.

[1] Naturally, it would be wrong to minimize the importance of the cult of the dead that comes out of the great magic tradition which is still alive in Homer's work. It constitutes the pivot of the *Iliad's* final episodes. But it has no influence whatever on the poet's philosophical thought.

Doubtless this is why neither of them grants mankind any pre-eminence. Because mankind does not die —at least to our limited vision—it is not superior to man. On the contrary, it is inferior to him, precisely in its lack of finiteness. Christianity has indeed exalted mankind, but only by restoring death to it in the person of Christ in whom the human race is incarnate.

Thus eternity belongs exclusively to that Being whom Tolstoy calls God and into which he tries to dissolve everything that has been delivered from the sin of individuation, and to which Homer, without naming it, gives an active solidarity with all perishable existence. This All, this Being, however, only manifests itself in a ceaselessly changing Becoming, whose irregular progression, made up of advances and retreats, seems to hide a creative aim. When the opposing armies face each other before Troy or Moscow, they are inditing together, beyond the inexpiable that separates them, the text of the epic from which men to come will extract the power of transforming the world. And this transfiguration is surely not a redemption. The treasures of life and consciousness that have been stupidly sacrificed to the routines of power cannot thus be requited or revived. But the summons of the irreparable awakes the creative will turned toward the future whence the answer must come. If there is any authentic solidarity or living communion between isolated individuals, does it not lie in the hope of constructing a new reality upon the foundation of injustice and sorrow?

When Homer and Tolstoy want to illuminate the fatality inherent in force—the inevitable glide of the creative will into the automatism of violence, of conquest into terror, of courage into cruelty—they do not fall into invective and moral indignation. An image suffices them, a contrast that remains forever present in our memories. The profound kinship between the Greek poet and the Russian poet is nowhere more clearly shown than in the fraternal resemblance between Petya, the cadet of the Rostov family, and Polydorus, Priam's youngest son. Both boys have been forbidden to go to war; lightly defying this prohibition, they outwit their guardians and leap into battle; there they are mowed down. To the mechanical unleashing of brutality, Homer and Tolstoy merely oppose the laughing grace of an adolescent for whom crossing the enemy lines is a kind of mimicry of the game of war. That same Achilles, who is in love with strife for its own sake, is not at all afraid to sully his glory by setting upon a weaponless child. Force is always the same, whether it subjects spirit to matter or matter to spirit. It identifies itself at the height of its curve with the creative gift; it transcends itself in the object it fashions, then subsides under its own law, exhausts itself, and breaks up. When Achilles, brutish with power, slaughters Polydorus and Lycaon, he is ripe for Paris' arrow.

In the spirit of equity, however, Homer infinitely surpasses Tolstoy. The Russian cannot restrain himself from belittling and disparaging the enemy of his people, from undressing him, as it were, before our eyes. The Greek does not humiliate either the victor or the vanquished; it is important to him that Achilles and Priam should do each other mutual homage. Since the guilt of Becoming weighs equally on men and gods, understanding and compassion must extend to the blessed as well as to the unfortunate, to Achilles as well as to Lycaon. Homer shows no preference or partiality for his own people; his model of human excellence is, after all, Hector, a Trojan. The spirit, here, is not fighting the battles of force, and hatred is unmixed with poison. Harshness and cruelty are part of the sport of war, and it does not occur to either side to make an agreement banning their use. The very desire for vengeance is a dazzling passion that hardens the will to victory; it is not a slow resentment that rots the soul. Opponents can do each other justice in the fiercest moments of combat; for them, magnanimity has not been outlawed. All this changes if the criterion of a conflict of force is no longer force but spirit. When war is seen as the materialization of a duel between truth and error, reciprocal esteem becomes impossible. There can be no intermission in a contest that pits—as in the Bible—God against false gods, the Eternal against the idol. This is a total war, which must be prosecuted on all grounds and in all weathers, till the extermination of the idol and the extirpation of the lie are accomplished. Under such conditions, to respect an opponent would be to pay homage to error and testify against truth.

For Tolstoy, Napoleon is not only the invader

of his country, but also God's rival; he is in the flesh
that great Figure who obstructs the return of particular existences to the indestructible Being. And
Kutuzov, too, is not only the hero-liberator of the
native soil, but also, even more forcibly, the anti-
hero, the modest interpreter of an historic necessity
whose significance and bearing confound the human
reason.

The style of the epic, when it attains the grandeur
it has in Homer and Tolstoy, demands an accurate
perception of true facts as well as the inclusiveness
of an all-embracing view; it has no place for the
arbitrary. It must give the sense of slowness and at
the same time have the gift of brevity; it must have
insight into collective states of mind and also into
individual souls; it must capture the cosmic vision and
be captivated by the anthropomorphic imagination;
any partiality of judgment or sensibility is therefore
impossible to it. The epic, in fact, demands of the
poet that he exercise the powers of the demiurge
and accord everything its rightful share, its full ex-
pressiveness; he must be guided by the profound
equity that the Creator shows to creation. In the
epic, the human plant is held out to us with particles
of earth still clinging to its roots; the hero does not
emerge from an indistinct mass but from a living
body of individuals in which Pierre Bezhukhov takes
his place beside Platon Karataev, in which Achilles
and Agamemnon keep their stature and their traits.

In Tolstoy and Homer, chastity as a power is not
sensuality's opposite but its most authentic manifes-

tation. It fortifies the will to expression while curb-ing emotivity: it is the dam that holds the waters to-gether in a pool where each interlaced design of foliage can mirror itself with its fretwork of sky. A hint, a flicker will catch the slightest tremor of sensation and leaves its purity unstained. Chastity is what gives this poetry its ability to describe the ex-treme with moderation and excess without excessive-ness, to plunge into the vortex of war and soar up into the peace of the constellations.

Priam and Achilles
Break Bread

W E REMEMBER the scene on which the *Iliad* ends: Priam has come to Achilles to reclaim his son's body. Prone at the feet of the victor, he assumes a majesty that does not derive from his office. By a new investiture, the king of Ilion has become "the king of suppliants."[1] From now on, this majesty is inviolable; in the calm that bathes total disaster, it rises above injury and attains to saintliness. "Have some awe of the gods, Achilles, and, remembering your own father, take pity on me. I am far more pitiable than he, for I have endured what no other mortal on earth has, to put to my mouth the hand of a man who has killed my sons." This speech is quite without vehemence; self-respect gives the words the exact weight

1 Péguy, *The Suppliants.*

97

of truth. In insisting on his right to pity, the vanquished is not bowing down to destiny in the person of the man he is entreating. The unheard-of ordeal he inflicts on himself, equal to the love that sustains him, has nothing base about it. Here, however, occurs an exceptional deviation from the laws of the mechanism of violence; this is the only case in the *Iliad* where supplication sobers the man to whom it is addressed instead of exasperating him. Suddenly it becomes plain that Achilles is just as much Achilles' victim as Priam's sons were. At the sight of the old king, to whom he has left nothing but the royalty of misfortune, the conqueror is struck dumb; he seems to come to himself and be cured of his frenzy. The old man's words arouse in him "the desire to mourn for his father." The killer is a man again, burdened with childhood and death. "He took the old man's hand and gently pushed him away. Both remembered. . . ." Here, I think, comes one of the most beautiful silences in the *Iliad*—one of those absolute silences in which the din of the Trojan War, the vociferations of men and gods, and the rumblings of the Cosmos, are engulfed. The Becoming of the universe hangs suspended in this impalpable element whose duration is an instant and forever.

If Priam today were to think of entreating Achilles, he would find Achilles no longer there. Outrage, bent on destruction, does not stop with the body or the soul. It insinuates itself into the very consciousness that the vanquished has of himself. It makes the victim ugly in his own eyes. It even dirties the pity one can feel for him. Humiliation, poisoned by the lie that the fact of force is wrapped in, has never before so eroded the inwardness of existence. Certainly the pact between force and fraud is as old as humanity. But at least it used to be possible to distinguish between the two. Achilles, even in his most inconsequential actions, refuses to let the two be confused. He eludes, to some extent, the definition Péguy gives of the man to whom supplications are addressed: ". . . a man who has what they call a fine position . . . one of the strong ones of the earth . . . a happy man, a man who appears to be and who *is* happy." One of the strong ones of the earth Achilles certainly is; yet he is far from being a happy man, in spite of all his prizes and rewards. Unlike Agamemnon, so clever at turning the grudges of his dangerous ally to his own advantage, he is not a chief of state; he is no fox, like Odysseus, patron saint of those wily traders whose audacity made Greece into a world. Nor is he one of those harsh Achaian lords whose strength is measured numerically by the herds and land they possess. Achilles has conquered, but he will not exploit his victories. It is Odysseus who will level Ilion, guardian of the routes to Asia and the barbarian seas. With Achilles, cruelty is not a technique, still less a method, but a sort of paroxysm of irritation in pursuit and counterstroke. It seems to be his only means of renewing the illusion of omnipotence which supplies him with his reason for living. The perfect conformity of his nature to his vocation of destroyer makes him the least free person there is; but it gives him in return a bodily freedom which is in itself a magnificent spectacle. One does not have to lower oneself to admire this "great proud soul" that is its own prisoner in a sovereign body. But if Priam admires Achilles, Homer does not tell us that he honors him. We do not see him in any way subjugated by the prestige of the hero, though misfortune has made him bow to him. He would certainly not set him as an example for his people or his sons.

During this strange pause arranged for him by destiny on the extreme edge of suffering, Priam delights in Achilles' beauty—the beauty of force. The soul, delivered from the bondage of events, substitutes the order of contemplation for the order of passion; it is a moment of sacred truce. Under the influence of grief, the atrocious reality had hardened into something stony; now it melts, becomes fluid and fleeting. Hatred is disconcerted and relents. The two adversaries can exchange looks without seeing each other as targets, as objects which there is merit in destroying. Thanks to this detachment, private life, the love of the gods and of earthly beauty, the frail and obstinate will of whatever defies death to flower and bear fruit—all those things that rage had trampled down—are reborn and breathe again. "Come now, sit upon a seat, and let sorrows rest in our minds, in spite of our pain. Chill grief is profitless," Achilles advises. At this moment, he is overwhelmed by compassion, though still remorseless. He lifts up the prostrate old man, comforts him, praises his courage, and never for a moment repents the evil he has done him and will continue to do him. Priam's job is to resign himself and endure his fate. Achilles himself is "an unhappy son doomed to die before his time," in exile. All men live in affliction: there is no other basis for true equality. Homer was anxious to have precisely the conqueror recall this fact to the conquered. To save the suppliant's honor, but also to rid himself of a troublesome responsibility, Achilles ducks behind fatality. Priam receives in silence the lesson read him by his son's murderer. He does not protest against such scandalous behavior. This "wisdom" does not shock and anger him, as it did Job. "How long wilt Thou afflict my soul and oppress me with Thy sermons?" Unlike Job, he does not have the resource of pleading his cause before God. Job can blame God who has despoiled him and who refuses him justice. "The Almighty is living who fills my soul with bitterness." But Priam remains silent when Achilles tenders him these counsels of resignation. Why get angry, justify oneself, come to one's own defense? Encircled by a stony fatality, he must turn to stone himself, like Niobe. Christianity was nurtured on Job's lament. It may owe more than we think to Priam's silence.

Achilles mistrusts himself. He is afraid that he will break this truce with one of his habitual outbursts. Consequently, he is careful not to give that side of his nature any pretext. "Priam must not see his son. At the sight of his son, in his grief of heart he might not be able to control his wrath, and Achilles, then, might be angered and kill him, thus violating Zeus's command." That is what he wants to avoid. Cautioned by Thetis, he consents to return to Priam his son's corpse. "From the countless ransoms provided for Hector's head," he detaches two pieces of linen, also a well-woven tunic. And when his female captives have washed the body of his enemy and anointed it with oil, "and have thrown over it, besides the tunic, a beautiful piece of linen, then Achilles himself lifts it and sets it upon a bier which his comrades with him lift onto the well-polished chariot." When this is done, he must weep again, and then apologize to Patroclus for putting an end to the reprisals—he promises him a fair share of the ransom offered for the murderer's body. His scruples put to rest, he calms himself, tells Priam that his son has been returned, and invites him to share his meal. "Let us think about eating, noble old man; later on you may lament your dear son, bringing him back to Ilion; he will get many tears from you." Priam does not refuse this meal, these funeral meats between life and death, this intermission of peace and communion between war and war. Homer never leaves out anything that shows how the body reacts to the changes of the soul. He knows the hunger of a man hollow by affliction—the body must take its just revenge on the exhausted soul before the soul can extort new tears from it. This nocturnal meal is no dream-meal, removed from the life of the flesh; it is a celebration of the things that surpass and sanctify the body's existence. "When they have banished thirst and appetite," Achilles and his guest relax and forget, or at least want to forget, the inexpiable. "Priam marvels at Achilles and finds him beautiful." Achilles, for his part, marvels at Priam and is struck by his noble appearance.

Here again beauty holds out for the sufferer a possibility of redemption. These pauses in the flux of Becoming, where beauty achieves translucence in the eternal, are not "beautiful moments" without moorings, having no ties to reality. They do not stand beyond time that beats out the furious rhythm of action. When Helen climbs the ramparts of Troy or when Priam enters Achilles' tent, these places become premises of truth, where *forgetfulness of an offense* in the contemplation of the eternal is made possible (pardon for an offense being unknown to the ancient world). Thus we find Homer already expressing, with a fullness unequalled by the philosophers, an intuition of the identity of truth and beauty that fructifies Greek thought.

Holding himself a little withdrawn, standing, as it were, at the crossroads between the tragic and the contemplative order, Priam appears in the epic like the poet's delegate, the incarnation of Homeric wisdom.[1] He typifies the watcher of tragedy, the man who sees it all, more completely and more truly than Zeus on Mount Ida because he is also a sufferer in the drama he is witnessing. Thanks to him, the prestige of weakness triumphs momentarily over the

---

[1] We do not realize that he dominates the poem until we have finished reading it.

prestige of force. When he admires the enemy who is crushing him and justifies the stranger whose presence is the ruin of his city, the old king gives absolution to life in its totality. In this minute of ecstatic lucidity, the haggard world recomposes its features, and the horror of what is to come is abolished in suffering hearts. It is useless to go beyond this. For Priam, the future is the burning of Troy, and for Achilles, it is Paris' arrow. Job will regain through faith all the treasures of the real world, but what Priam is about to recover is only Hector's corpse. Yet out of this encounter on the borders of night comes a dawn of joy, unknown to joy, that reconciles life to itself. Niobe awakes and stretches her petrified limbs.

Achilles does not stop with carrying out the gods' orders. He goes farther and promises Priam to suspend the battle and hold the army in check until Hector's funeral is over. Then, with tenderness and respect, with that infinite delicacy that is the adjunct of true force, "he takes the old man by the wrist, lest he should fear in his mind."

This, then, is Achilles, more like Alexander or the great Condé than like the barbarians he descends from. His courtliness alone, apparent in the grace of his welcome, betrays a man of high lineage in whom brutality threatens an already high-wrought civilization. We must not forget that this disillusioned conqueror has a passion for music. Odysseus finds him at his *cythara* when he comes with his embassy to try to mollify him, the "beautiful, curiously wrought *cythara"* that he seized for his own use from the spoils of a city he destroyed. "His heart delighted in touching it and he was singing the exploits of heroes." We must not forget about this song. Friendship and music are Achilles' only deliverance. But is it deliverance that he really wants? The glory he has chosen in preference to a long life is the immortality of omnipotence, not the immortality of the soul. It would be possible to see in Achilles the Dionysiac strain, a passion for destruction growing out of a hatred for the destructibility of all things; and in Hector, the Apollonian part, the will toward preservation growing out of love for human achievements in their vulnerability. It would be possible, except for the fact that Homer's characters are infinitely more complex than we suspect if we let the concentration and voluntary abbreviation of the classic style lead us astray.

Close study of the poem's composition is an endless labor. Clarity multiplies the enigmas; the precision of the strokes emphasizes the evasiveness of life. Beneath the marvellous unity of the form, the ambiguity of the real comes to life again. The great symmetries of Becoming are respected and kept in focus throughout, but they only reveal more distinctly the presence of something incommensurable. Things that seem as if they ought to defy, by their very nature, plastic sculptural treatment—the furtive, the fleeting, the teeming of possibilities, the mirror play of contrasts—get incorporated into these statues somehow, by some miraculous process, and the calm of the statues is not for an instant disturbed. Homer's heroes appear to us in relief, as actors on the tragic scene; at the same time, however, they wear the halo of mortal existences. "To be a classic," says Nietzsche, "one must have *all* the gifts and *all* the needs, but one must force them all under the same yoke." And it might be Homer to whom Nietzsche is referring when he asserts that the greatness of the classic artist is measured by "the infallible sureness with which chaos obeys and takes form at the sound of his voice, at the necessity his hand expresses in a series of forms."

Poets and Prophets

THE sense of the true is always a kind of conquest, but first it is a gift. There are other sacred texts besides the Bible and the *Iliad*, but none in which justness of thought seems more plainly a vocation. Elsewhere we are on foreign soil; here we are on native ground; here we purify ourselves at our sources. By some insensible process of growth, the Bible and the *Iliad* always encompass our experience at its richest and most contradictory. They offer us what we most thirst for, the contact of truth in the midst of our struggles. The more intimate our commerce with these two divinely inspired books, the more suspicious we become of symbolic interpretations that charge them with too rich a meaning. Is it too venturesome to find some profound identity between Biblical thought and Homeric thought, an identity that lies deeper than the contrasts between the courage of righteous action and the heroism of martial action, between salvation by faith and redemption through poetry, between eternity proclaimed as the future life and the timeless eternity made actual in a perfect form? Certainly the heroes who eclipse their protector gods by attracting all the light of destiny to themselves have nothing in common with the sinful nation that devotes its substance to enriching the unique God. Still, the religion of *Fatum* and the worship of the living God both involve a refusal to turn man's relation to the divine into a technique or a mystical formula. The God of the Bible can be touched but not suborned by prayers; propitiatory rites are capable of appeasing the Olympians but not of deflecting *Fatum*.

Nothing is more foreign to the God of Israel than the impassible detachment of the mystics' deity. He does not expect his creatures to set aside the richness of the concrete so as to be open to Him. Nor does He retain for Himself the privilege of escaping the struggle and effort He has imposed upon mankind. Moses is punished for having yielded to the pressure of the people, who insisted that he turn his intimacy with God into a magical relationship to the occult. Prometheus is not only the victim of his creative audacity and redemptory devotion; he is also expiating his boastfulness, his presumptuous attempt to free man from the laws of his condition by the use of science and magic.

With the prophets and the tragic poets, the religious intuition of truth rests, then, on an acceptance of non-power reached only when thought itself becomes most powerful and most passionate. Radical disenchantment is just as bitter in the psalms of David as in the threnodies of Homer and Aeschylus, though, in the one case, jubilation surmounts it and, in the other, mourning consecrates it. However distant the love of God may be from the *Amor fati,* both achieve ultimate humility in the acceptance of what is, in truth, a scandal—the incommensurability of ethical categories with the action of a just god in history. Job argues and accuses, but God, like the *Fatum,* does not justify Himself. The prophets of Israel glorify a Lord who annihilates whole generations to recreate a people who will be capable of receiving His gifts. The heroes of the *Iliad* attain their highest lucidity at a point when justice has been utterly crushed and obliterated. But the renunciation of all hope of retribution does not kill the passion for eternity. This still lives; indeed, it shows itself more tenacious than ever in Hector's resolution: "Well, no, I do not intend to die without a struggle, nor without glory, nor without some high deed, the tale of which will reach the ears of men to come." It burns in the Psalmist's cries of exultation: "I will sing unto the Lord as long as I live; I will sing praise to my God while I have my being." He knows the nothingness of all the sons of man, and defies death none the less for it. He has the hardiness to sustain the contrast between the limitations of created beings and "the limitless commandment of God."

Both the Bible and the *Iliad* link ethical experience and metaphysical questioning very closely. The ambiguous universe of demoniac forces is just receding from view; the world of rational symbols has not yet been constituted. Magic no longer possesses anything but ineffectual rites to impose on recalcitrant nature, and philosophy has still to invent its own incantations for bringing beautiful abstractions to life. At this possibly privileged moment, in the lyric preaching of the prophets of Israel and in the epic of Homer, a particular mode of thought is evolved which cannot be expressed and transmitted to successive generations in conceptual form, but which reappears and holds good every time man comes up against himself at the dark turn of his existence.

Correspondingly, there is no line of connection between the spirit of the Bible and religious spiritualism or between the spirit of the *Iliad* and philosophic spiritualism. The *Fatum* of the epic bears no more resemblance to the immutable essences of the philosophers than the God of Moses bears to the god of the deists or the theosophists. There is nothing more severely human, and less humanitarian, than this inspired thought that never gets away from the oscillations of subjectivity. But the more it embraces individual reality the less individualist it is.

The prophets lay down a policy for the conduct of a small nation exposed to the encroachments of its formidable neighbors. It must be ready to fight on some occasions, and on others it must lie patient under the oppressor's yoke without losing its desire for independence and its faith in its own destiny. This policy is remarkably expert at finding the vulnerable point of great empires; it is quick to detect the weakness that is hidden by prestige. And Homer, too, the first of the Greek historians, provides a lucid analysis of the political and economic causes of the conflict that opposed the militarism of the arrogant Achaian peasants to the pacifism of the Trojan "plutocracy." But when historical exposition has exhausted the last detail of the facts and analyzed all the causes, it leaves us at the door of the event—it stops short of war, of the irrational, short, in fact, of Achilles. Thought, with Homer and the prophets, always darts beyond social ends to Being itself or to the religious affirmation of life in its totality. The very notion of nationalism is as foreign to the Bible (where the nation is only exalted insofar as it has been summoned by God) as to Homer, whose impartiality achieves such a degree of merciful understanding that we have to give up trying to find out the personal preferences of the poet. What we have, rather, is a form of thought essentially ethical, if this word is used merely to designate the experience of total distress where the very absence of choice compels us to choose. "Inwardness lasts only an instant," says Kierkegaard. The thought of the Bible and of Homer feeds on these instants, even when it seems to plunge downward into history.

The crises which disrupt the individual do not alter the constants of human Becoming. History remains a tangled succession of catastrophes and breathing spaces, of problems provisionally set, resolved, or conjured away. But the man who has felt the terrible pressure of total impotence and survived that experience does not resign himself to living as if this had never happened to him. He tries to keep hold of the supreme resources revealed to him by despair. He tries to integrate the subjective intensity of such moments to the continuity of his existence, to capure spontaneity through repetition. The step from ethics to morality involves the same betrayal of value as the descent from esthetic contemplation to hedonism: the ethical quality, which has no degrees, debases itself in order to become a moral quality susceptible of being evaluated in terms of comparison. One tries, then, to obtain through discipline a style of life that will perpetuate the memory of these instants of inwardness. But as soon as subjectivity drops from its momentary exaltation to its normal level, it loses its capacity for transcending itself, and of its transformation retains only a feeble image. Just as esthetic contemplation is never complete outside a work of art, so the ethical experience lives only in the acts that embody it. What would remain of this experience if poetry did not bear witness to its reality? What would become of its permanence if it were not assisted by creative imagination and verbal genius that accomplish on the plane of poetry the miracle of impossible repetition? Thus the bond that attaches ethics to poetry is infinitely more profound and more solid than the bond that shackles ethics to morality. If the religion of the Bible and the religion of *Fatum* both resort to poetry in order to communicate with the people, this is because poetry gives them back the truth of the ethical experience on which they are based. When Nietzsche proclaims his Dionysiac faith in the Eternal recurrence, when Blake describes his vision, when Kierkegaard wants to puzzle out Abraham's experience, and Pascal to acknowledge the God of Abraham and Jacob, it is on the language of poetry —on aphorism and paradox—that they all must rely.

The climate of the *Iliad* is no more favorable than that of the Bible to the diffuse eroticism that sustains the workings of magic. A new energy has come along to collect the scattered Eros of nature divinities into one powerful love. Yet the attraction of the perishable, the spell of sensation remain. A grand anthropomorphic imagination forges a new bond between the individual and the universe, sanctifying the relationship of man to the elemental forces. Mountains and islands, rivers and springs join in the praise of God or enlist in the struggles of the heroes. An inexhaustible animality extending from man to nature is being transmuted into the most delicate feelings. Thus, under the harsh sun, grows the friendship between Achilles and Patroclus, between David and Jonathan.

How much the interpenetration of poetic and religious values contributes to the liberation of the individual conscience can be surmised if we look to see what happens to them once they have been severed from each other. When the prodigious inspira-

tion of prophetic poetry runs dry, the religion of
the Bible degenerates into a febrile messianic mysticism. When rationalism undertakes to substitute its
own answers for the questions of Homer and
Aeschylus, tragic ethos becomes Stoicism. Morality
hushes the plaint of the hero—groans are an unseemly
noise.

Faith is not the only agency that disposseses magic
and installs ethics in its place at the heart of existence:
poetry, too, steals its thunder—warriors' exploits sup-
plant the exploits of mythical heroes; the story of
God's action, in the Bible, does not tolerate the
presence of other wonders beside it. For the first
time, myth loses its magic properties, its social virtue,
and its explanatory value. While no longer assuming
its traditional functions, it has not yet acquired the
philosophical significance which Plato will impart to
it later.

Recourse to myth, with Plato, is a kind of free
play of the creative imagination which disguises the
helplessness of reason before its own paradox. Truth
here is mocking truth, while the passion for knowledge takes a breathing spell and falls back on the old
animism as a method of explanation. Plato's myths
are images of existence in which irony triumphs over
spirit of pedantry. In them, he is certainly acknowl-
edging the powerlessness of reason, but is he not also,
in this very act, coming to reason's rescue? When
reason can go no further, he lets myth take over.
Philosophy never disdains any alliance that will help
it extend its domain over man and the universe. There

are times when demons and ideas do not make such bad companions. Plato is never troubled by the incompatibility of animism with the principles and methods of his philosophy. The truth is that reasoning and syllogistic operations, incantation and exorcistic formula are all heading toward the same end but using different routes. It is only natural then that Plato should not hesitate to ground his rational constructions on a mythical base or to confiscate for reason's benefit the sense of awe and holy conviction that clings to certain collective representations. Myth as interpreter of the invisible world and mediator between the sensible and the intelligible tempts both the philosopher and the seer in Plato.

But it is precisely both the magical and the philosophical ambitions that the Bible and the *Iliad* exclude. Prophecy debars divination and is not attained by magical procedures. Straightness of heart is the only means of making contact with the beyond. This beyond, as a matter of fact, is absent from the *Iliad*. Homer and Aeschylus would have been able to see through the gods to God, had His place not been occupied by *Fatum*. The *Amor fati*, not polytheism was the real obstacle to faith for the ancients. But Homer is quite as hard as the Bible on human pride and the will to omnipotence. In the paroxysm of martial action, the hero is endowed with superhuman powers, but they only expose him to implacable reprisals. The gods accord their protégés a brief invulnerability that makes the precariousness of force

in its short-lived assurance all the more apparent.
However, the belief in *Fatum* and the religion of
the One God do not either of them involve that
depreciation of the perceptual world to which all
philosophy commits us under cover of a respect for
value. A boundless tenderness for perishable things
torments the hearts of men wrenched from their true
goods. But this *wrenching*, whether it is the effect
of God's punishment or of *Fatum's* decrees, has nothing in common with *unbinding*, with the separation
of body and soul considered desirable by the philosophers. The prophets' love for the oppressed nation,
Prometheus' love for the threatened human race, does
not depart from its object to seize hold of the eternal.
God "on high," "whom the heaven of heavens cannot contain," lives with man on earth. Humility before the real, before untamable existence, is what we
learn from the grief and supplications of the tragic
poets and the exhortations and lamentations of the
prophets. It is proper, then, to distinguish the ethical
thought of the Bible and the *Iliad* from the magical
thought that preceded it and the dialectical thought
that was to follow it. Some affinity, however, might
be conceded between Plato's metaphysics and the
meditations of Isaiah or Homer. Is not Socrates' wish
for immortality already fulfilled in those contemplative pauses of the *Iliad*? The God of the Bible is not
always flaming in the Burning Bush. He passes also
"in the most furtive breeze." At such moments, does
He not fan with His breath the "marvelous hope" of
Plato?

As it manifests itself in the Homeric universe, split into a plurality of antagonistic energies that hold each other in check, its image multiplied in the duels of the warriors and the quarrels of the gods, force appears homogeneous in its principle, identical with the Becoming that determines it, without origin and without end. It is what is, firstly, indefinitely, absolutely. In the Biblical universe, on the contrary, the representation of force implies a fundamental if not original heterogeneousness—in its finite aspect, force is the will to power which man makes into a god; in its infinite aspect, it is God. Opposing corruptible energy to creative energy, the Bible maintains a duality which it only overleaps in the idea of resurrection. Obviously, then, the conception of force is what initially conditions the Greek belief in an intemporal immortality and Israel's belief in the resurrection. In the latter, Becoming is the image of redemption on the march toward a moving end; in the former, Becoming presents itself as a tangled succession of growths, evolutions, and deaths, athwart which the permanence of Being affirms itself. In the Bible, God is master of Becoming; in the *Iliad*, Becoming, or *Fatum*, if you wish, is master of the gods.

The idea of resurrection brings temporality sharply to the fore; Biblical religion is emphatically not a faith in immortality but a desire to destroy death in time. The nation is restored to life in God, and God also is restored to life in the nation's heart. Ethics itself is felt primarily as an *instant of resurrection* where man and God triumph together over decay. The monistic conception of force, on the other hand, the idea of the diffuse guilt, the image of *Fatum* and eternal Becoming, all this was bound to orient Greek thought along the path of esthetic detachment, intemporal eternity, and redemption through beauty. Long before it laid hold on Plato, the passion for the indestructible burst forth in Homer. With him begins the quest for perfection in which the asceticism and saintliness of the Greek genius are specially manifest. Homer, too, turns toward the future, but he does not locate a messianic peace there, the product of blood and horror. Rather, he hears in it the tranquil ecstasy of a song, whose consoling beauty will testify to squandered suffering by telling its truth.

Whereas faith in the Resurrection affirms the principle of communion, joining each individual member of the chosen people, then each nation, and at last the human race to God, in universal salvation, belief in immortality consecrates the principle of oneness, exalts the incomparable event—named Hector, or Achilles, or Helen—that emerges from Becoming for a single instant and forever. Man immortalizes the object of his love, and this function of his is the loftiest reason for his activity. God does just the opposite: He creates out of nothing and restores the dead to life. He is Ezekiel's God who pulls His people out of the sepulcher and blows on dead bones to make them live.

The demand for justice is related to the conception of force. Hence the prophet's attitude with respect to justice will differ from that of the Sage. The one hopes for justice from God alone; the other looks to the best part of himself for it—seeing it as the highest gift that man can make to man. From the point of view of the prophets, justice could not possibly sustain itself by its own powers. God has to help His people hammer it out in the great confusion of history, extract it from the chaos of iniquity. And when this people shows itself unworthy of election, the punishment that overtakes it falls on the just and the unjust alike (properly speaking, there are no innocent people in a guilty nation). The judgments of God are inscribed in the history of a people rather than in that of individuals; and there they can best be deciphered. Job will die, venting his stubborn complaint, but the nation can await the promised resurrection. "I will bear the wrath of the Lord because I have sinned against Him, until He defends my cause and does me justice." It has plenty of time to win justice—the whole span of the succession of generations, the whole length of the chain of disasters and miracles that constitutes its life. Consequently, the more misfortune pursues their people, the more strength the prophets find within themselves to refuse fatality the tribute of adoration conceded it by the Greeks.

For the Greeks, history is simply the stage of the tragedies of force and the dramas of collective passion; it has no awareness of divine justice and makes no appeal to it. Although the gods are involved in the unfolding of events through their participation in the conflicts of history, the whole business of founding and building, rising and daring, remains in the hands of man. Law is an altogether human work, a fragile bridge more durable, however, than it looks, as the swell of the passions sweep it without submerging it. If it falls to pieces, the great lawmaker is there, ready to do it over and perfect it. He is working on the foundations of the just city, trying to make them solid. The harshness of Creon is as alien to him as Antigone's intransigeance; he negotiates with life, knowing its suppleness and inflexibility. He tries to bend it to the commandment of justice, and justice to the commandment of necessity. He deals in compromise, to be sure, but bold compromise between two colliding absolutes.

Perhaps the great lawmaker, rather than the philosopher, is the legitimate heir to the Homeric wisdom and Hector's next-in-line. Solon, who was statesman, business man, soldier, traveller, legislator, and poet all at once, illustrates in his own person the close union between esthetic exigency and ethical incentive that is at the source of the Greek need for justice. In him we see the man of large experience, at home in war and peace, in whom the passion for balance is as strong as the passion for combat.

The gods bestow happiness, wealth, and glory. Man alone has the power to unite them to justice.

If he fails to do this, "fatal calamity" will overwhelm him sooner or later. "It begins small," says Solon, "like fire: first it is nothing; in the end, it is a great evil. The works of violence cannot endure. Zeus sees the term of all things. As the spring breeze, all at once, scatters the haze, and, having shaken the waves of the unfruitful sea, ravaging the rich fields of the nourishing earth, rises suddenly again toward the gods' high dwelling, toward the precipitous sky, and lets man see the ethereal splendor—then the force of the sun sheds its fair sparkling rays on the fat earth and all the clouds are vanished—so the vengeance of Zeus manifests itself." But if vengeance belongs to Zeus, the construction of just laws is mortals' task. Concern for justice remains man's secret pride before the anarchy of the gods, the cosmic disorder, the instability of human societies. Thus, with the Greeks, the taste for well-made laws is in keeping with the passion for independence and particularism. This passion may seem to be in contradiction with the universality of the *ius;* nevertheless, it quickens the will to justice.

However alien and mutually opposed the pathos of the Jewish prophet and the ethos of the Greek law-maker may appear to us, we can see from the exigency common to both that the roots of their conceptions touch. For both, justice, as man has received it from God, or as he cultivates it in the light of his own genius, is a fruit of the fructified earth: it can only begin its growth on the native soil. Later on, it can be grafted on other trunks and prosper in new climates. But in universalizing itself, it will never become a construction of the abstract reason, uniformly applicable in all times and places. Whenever it is transplanted, it will have to remake its growth and its maturation. When Hosea urges men to clear a new field of holiness, his appeal must be understood in a literal as well as a figurative sense. To sow according to justice and reap according to mercy, you must first sow and reap: "every man under his own vine and fig tree." God is the true proprietor of the native soil, from which the people get only the usufruct.

Renan would have us believe that the Jewish prophet was an agitator ("Loose the bonds of wickedness . . . undo the heavy burdens . . . let the oppressed go free . . . and break every yoke," Isaiah 58:6). But this is as untrue of the prophet as it is of the Greek lawmaker who "joining force to justice, . . . set free those who trembled before their masters." Listen to the prophet, and what you hear is the grand, energetic reproach of the man of the soil rising against enslavement, not the feverish recriminations of the deracinated person. Isaiah's social doctrine comes remarkably close to the teachings of Solon. When Solon wants to glorify his own handiwork, the wonderful constitution which combines hardihood with restraint, he calls Earth herself to witness: "She will bear witness well for me before the seat of Justice, grandmother of the Olympian gods, black Earth whose boundaries I have just now lifted, planted on all sides, a slave formerly and now

free. . . . I have written laws that are the same for
the miscreant and for the upright man, ordering for
all a very straight justice." In this cult of straightness,
that is, of equity, Jewish lawmakers and Athenians
meet.

Thus, for Athens as for Jerusalem, there is no
irreducible antagonism between human justice, rest-
ing on equity and truth (whether arrived at by faith
or by reason), and the justice of life which has no
other foundation than the physical and physiological
conditions under which an individual or a group can
flourish. The just man, in Athens or Zion, knows no
inner division when he finds himself surrounded by
adversaries. Anything that is beneficent for life cannot be injurious to God; anything that fructifies faith
cannot be injurious to life. "That which is altogether
just thou shalt follow, that thou mayest live and
inherit the land which the Lord thy God giveth thee."
Justice and life call out to each other across the
chasm of destruction and blend in creative activity.
If justice is realized according to divine prescription,
"The Lord thy God shall bless thee in all thine increase and in all the works of thine hands, therefore
thou shalt surely rejoice." Even when the guilty
nation drops to its scorched fields, stricken by the
"great, strong, harsh sword of the Eternal," it does
not lose faith in its land, which can restore shadows
to life.

But what could be more Greek, more essentially
Athenian, than this solidarity of justice and joy on
an earth set free by free men? Transcendent justice

and justice immanent in life do not always coincide; the lawmaker's task is to reduce the interval that separates them to a minimum. Yet in the end they do meet: in the final analysis, you cannot trample on one without destroying the other. "Contempt for law," says Solon, "covers the city with ills. When law reigns . . . it smoothes away rudeness, stifles pride, quenches violence, and withers calamity in the bud." This Greek eudaimonism is not so far as it seems from the eudaimonism of the Bible. In both, a love of country is extolled which combines the sense of the true and the taste for the just.

Christianity effected a tremendous synthesis between messianic religion and the mystic philosophies that were prevalent in Greece at a time when the distance between Judaism and Hellenism was most considerable. But to find the common ground of Greek and Jewish thought, one must look further back, to the great lyrics of Judaism, to Homer and the tragic poets. There are more real affinities between Hesiod's robust pessimism and Hosea's bracing acerbity, between Theognis' revolt and Habakkuk's apostrophes, between Job's lamentations and Aeschylus' threnodies, than between Aristotle and the Gospel. A synthesis of these pure elements would not have been possible or desirable. But there is and will continue to be a certain way of telling the truth, proclaiming the just, of seeking God and honoring man, that was first taught us and is taught us afresh every day by the Bible and by Homer.